Farmhouse
Simple Pleasures

TO:

FROM:

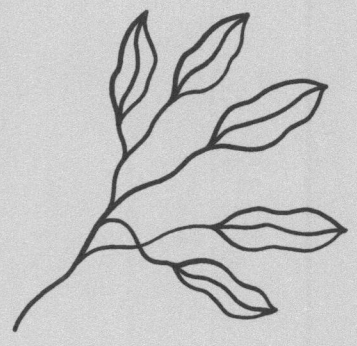

Copyright © 2021

All Rights Reserved. No part of this publication may be reproduced, distributed, or transmitted in any form or by any means, including photocopying, recording, or other electronic or mechanical methods, without the prior written permission of the author.

While most styles come and go, Farmhouse decor continues to stand the test of time by simply evolving.

The natural rustic hues allow me a special joy and pleasure.

~ Joy Visante

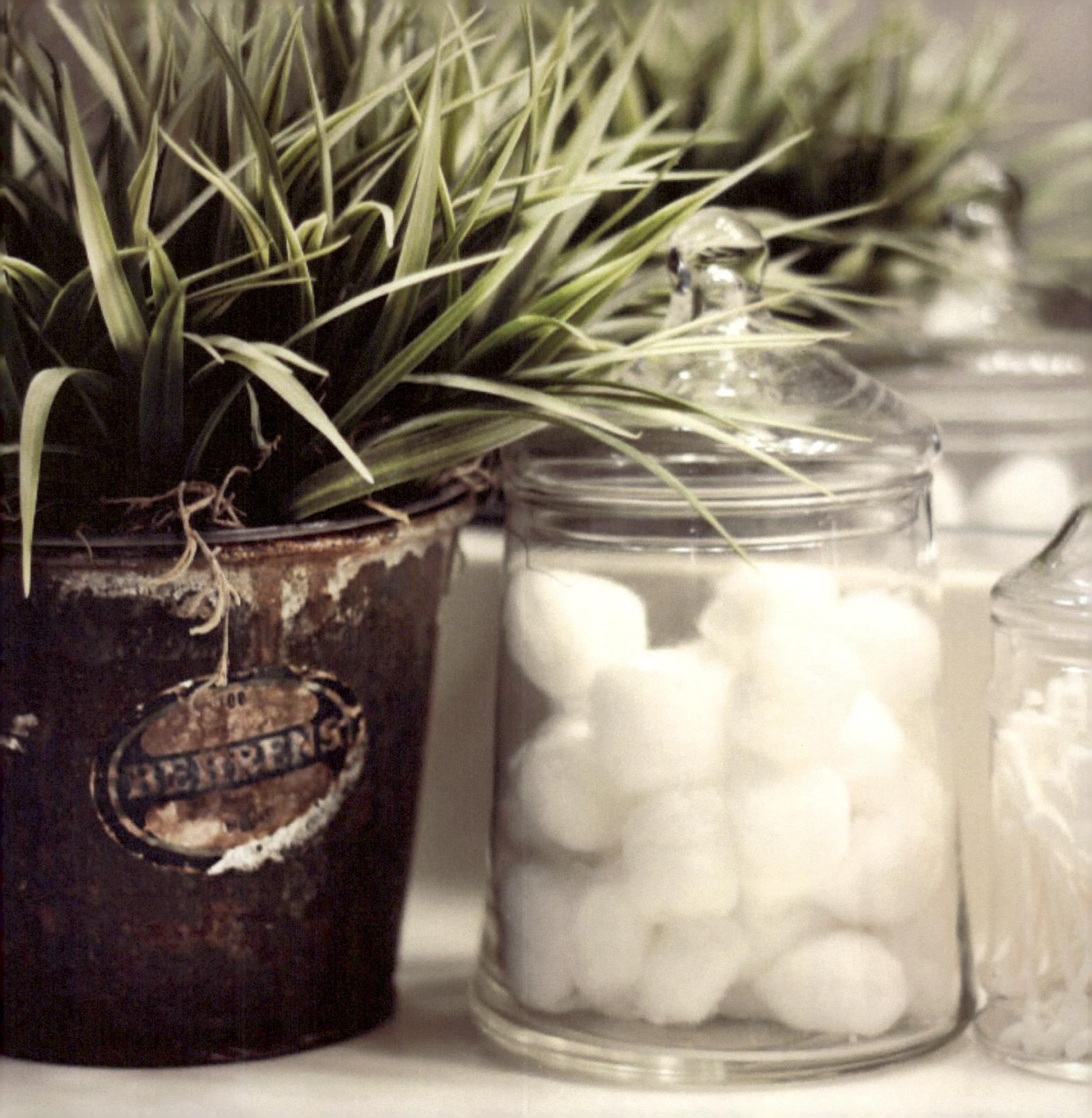

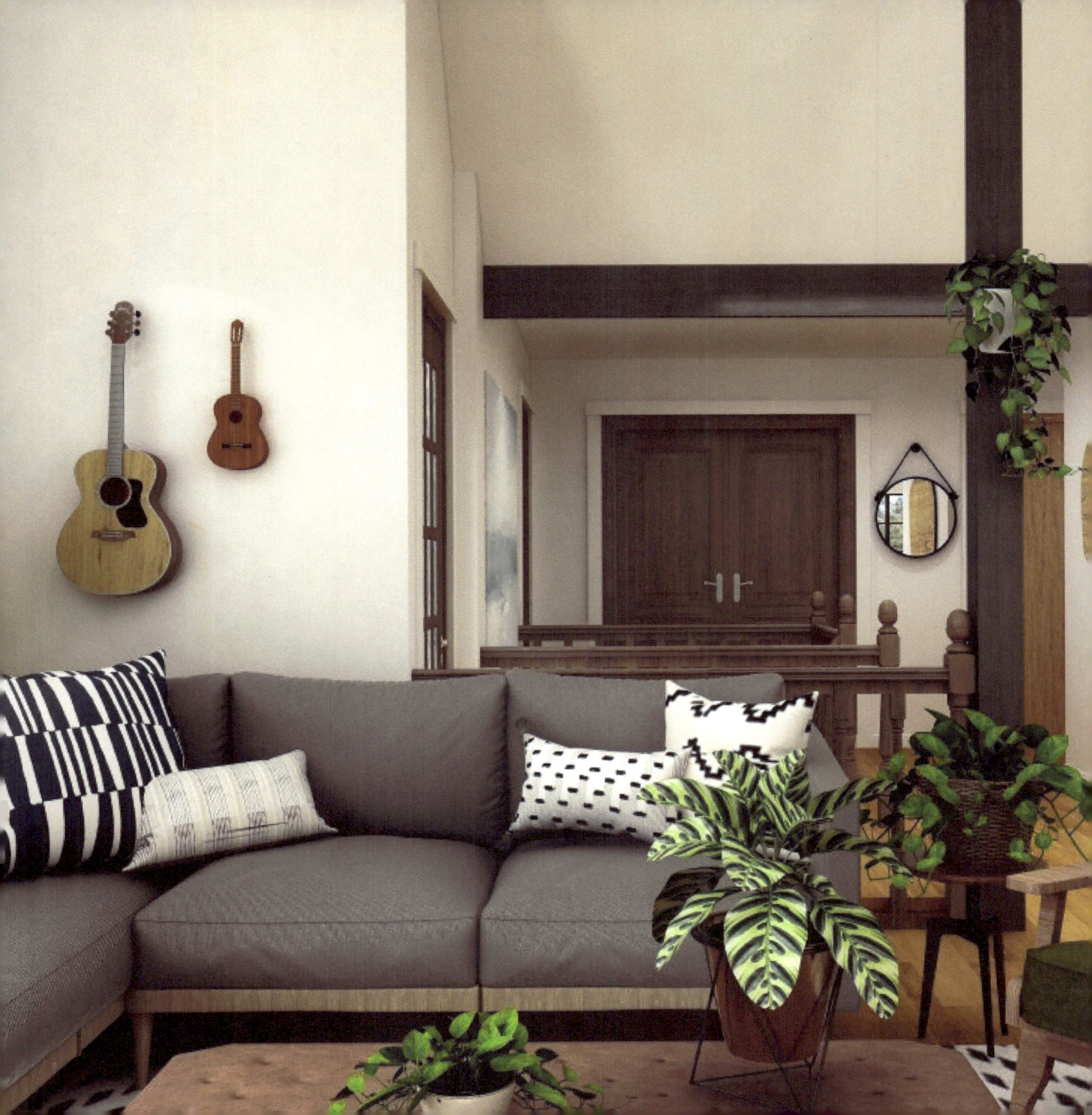

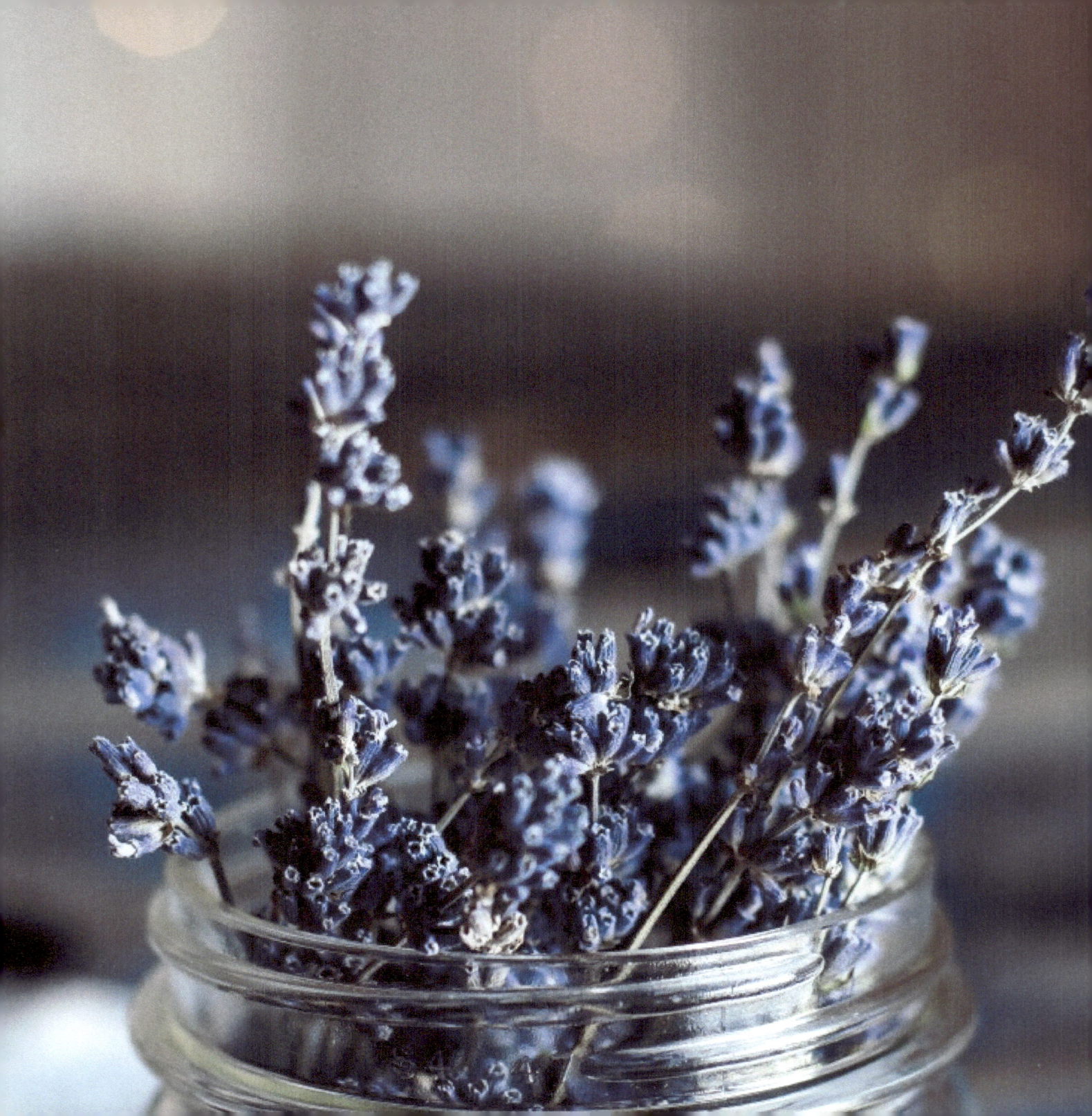

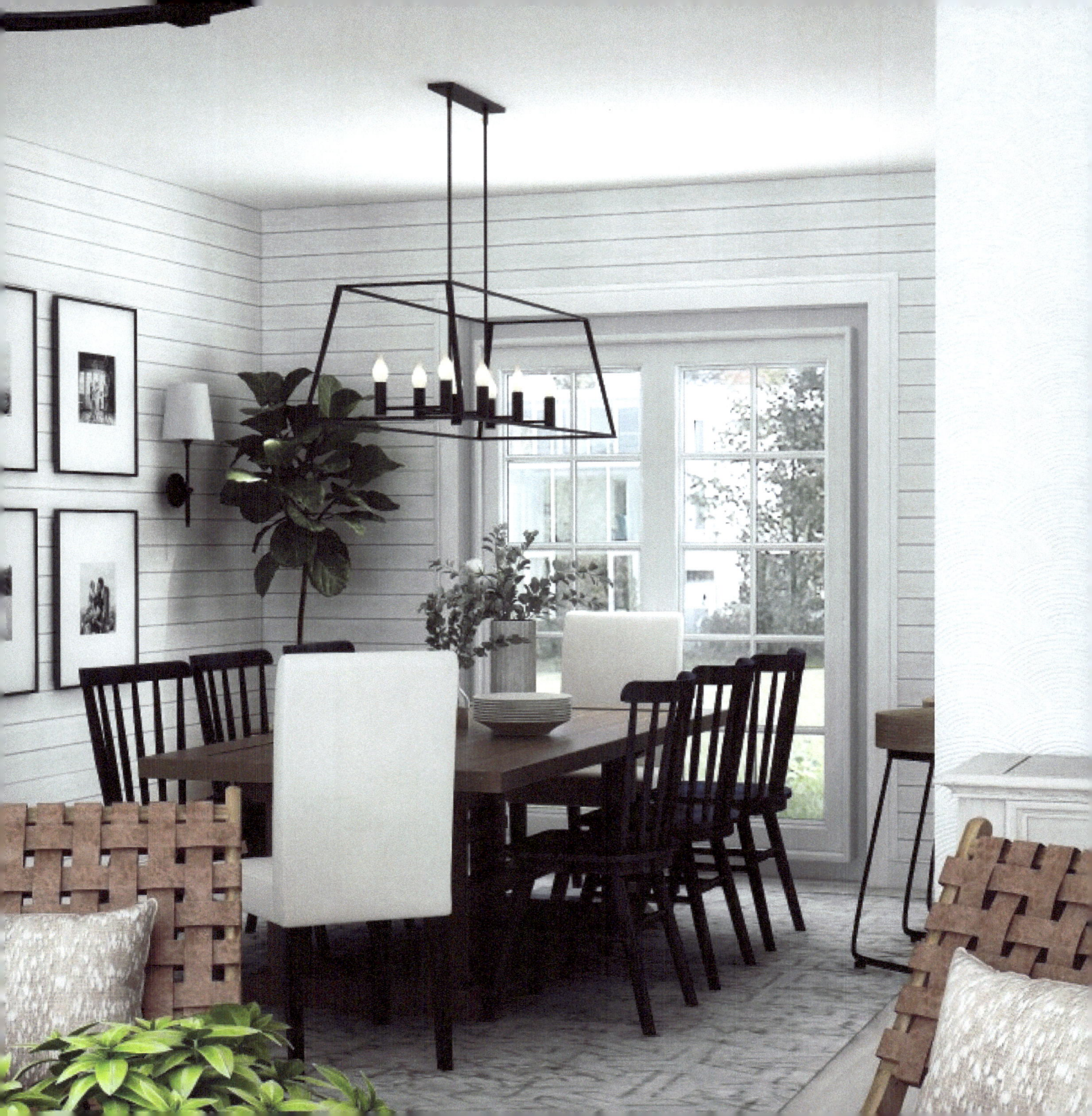

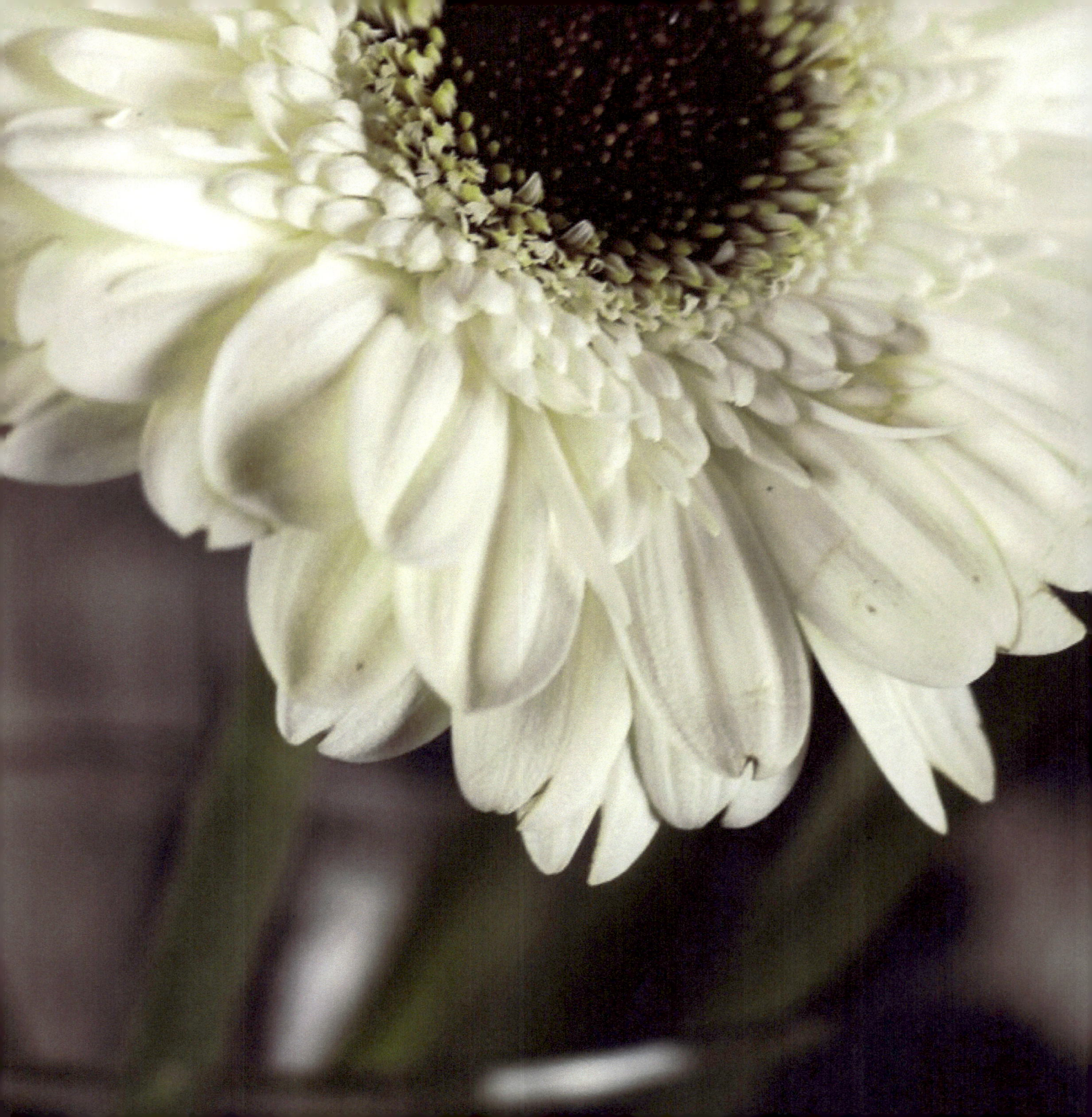

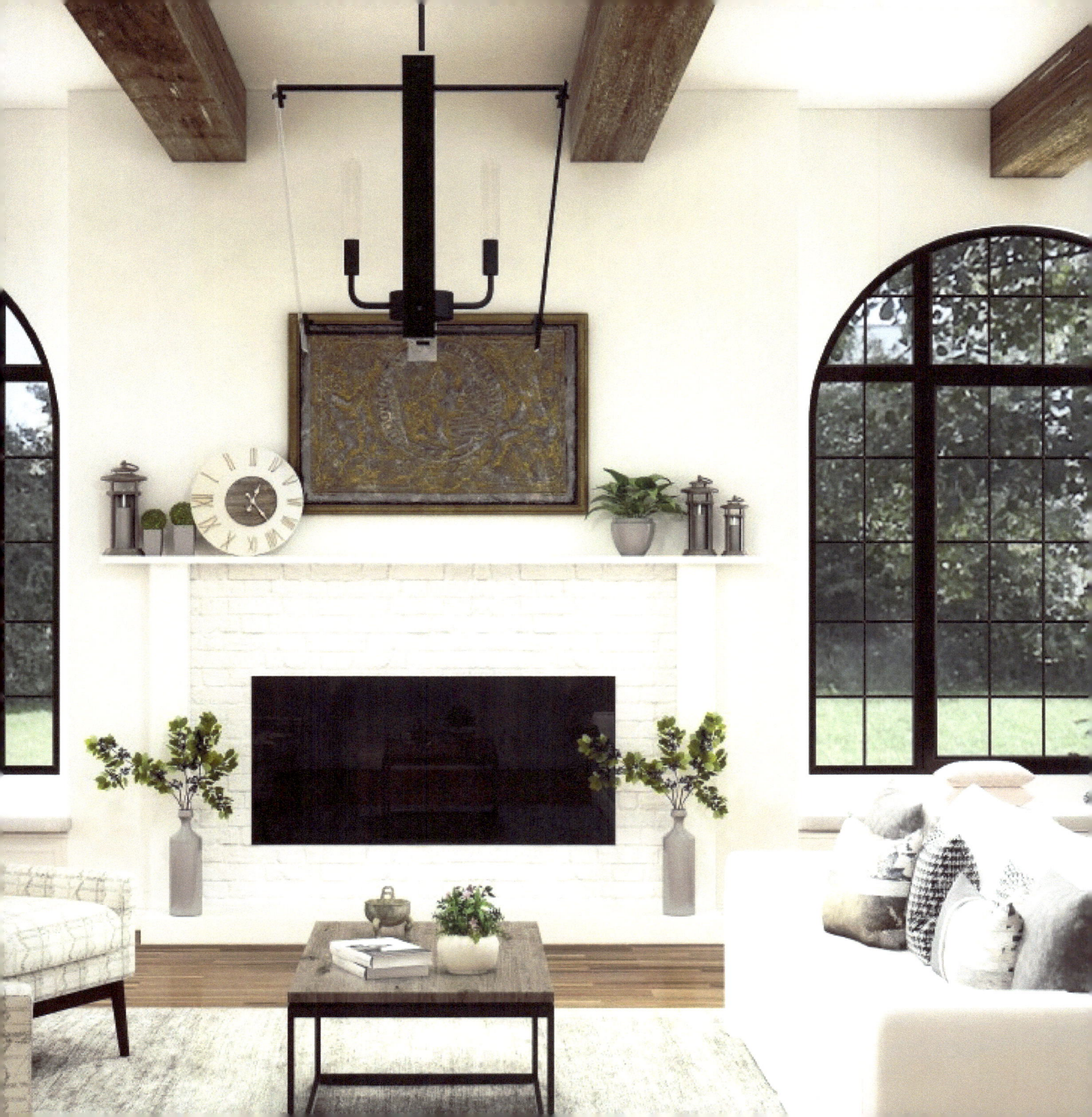

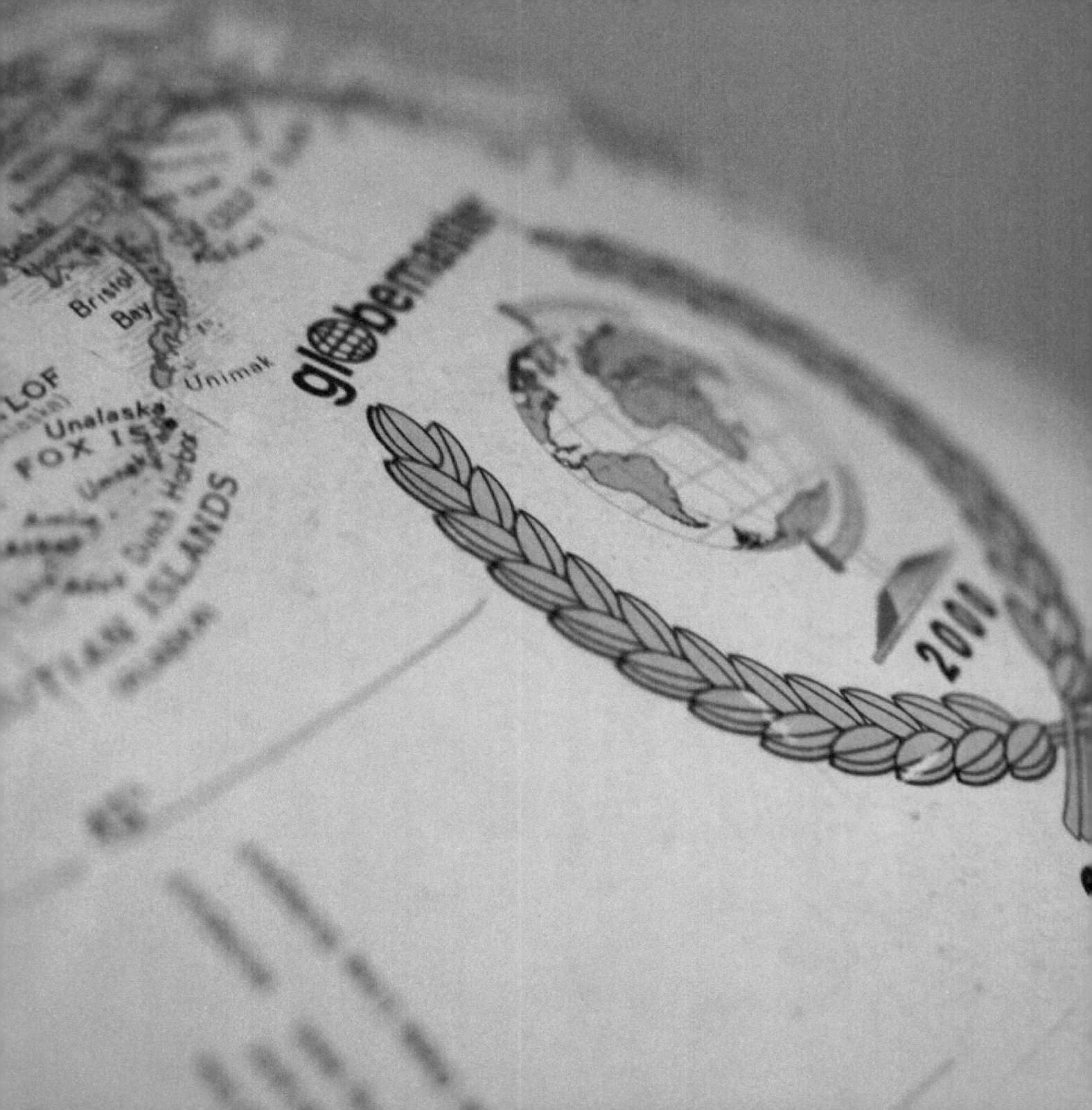

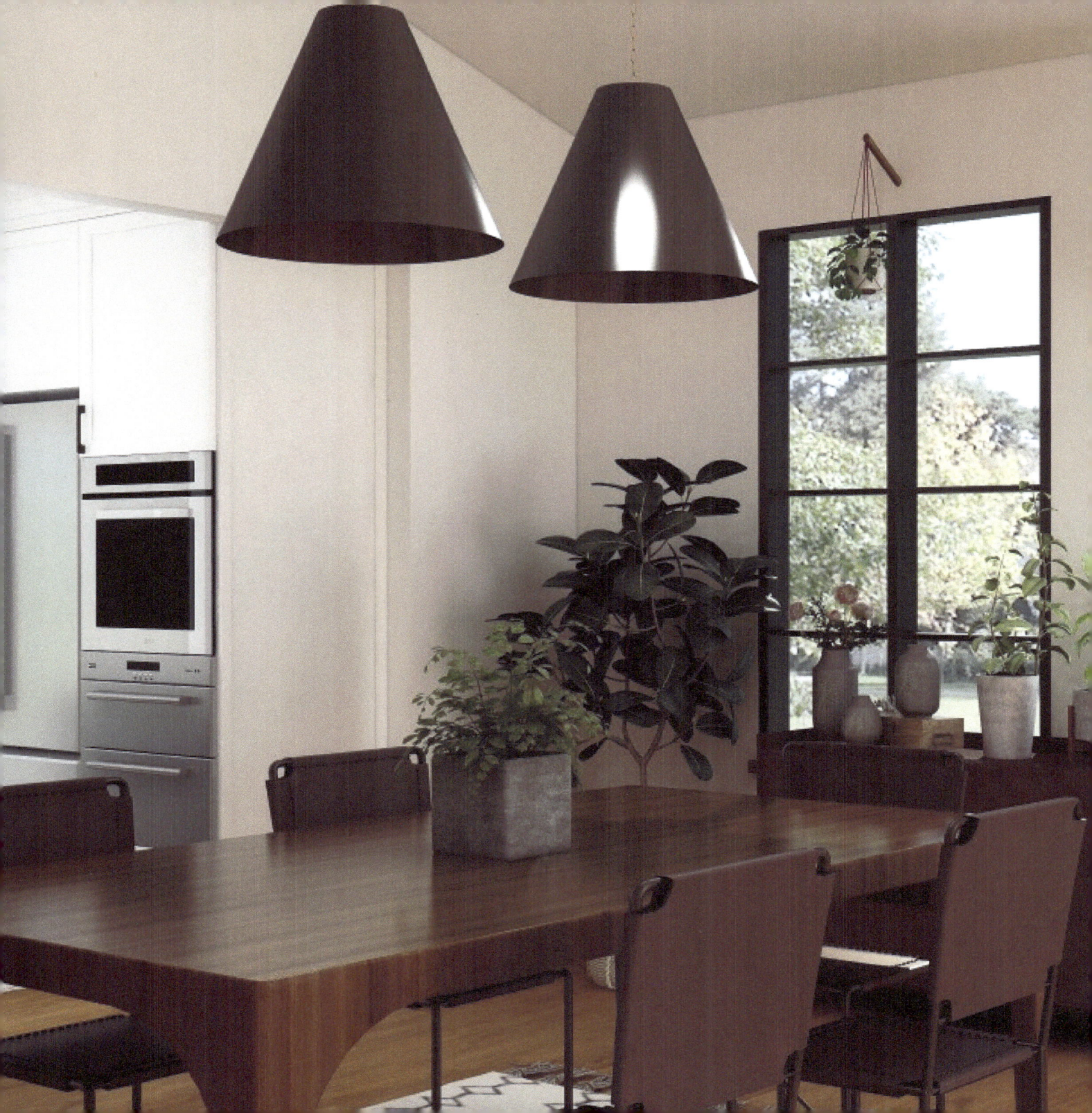

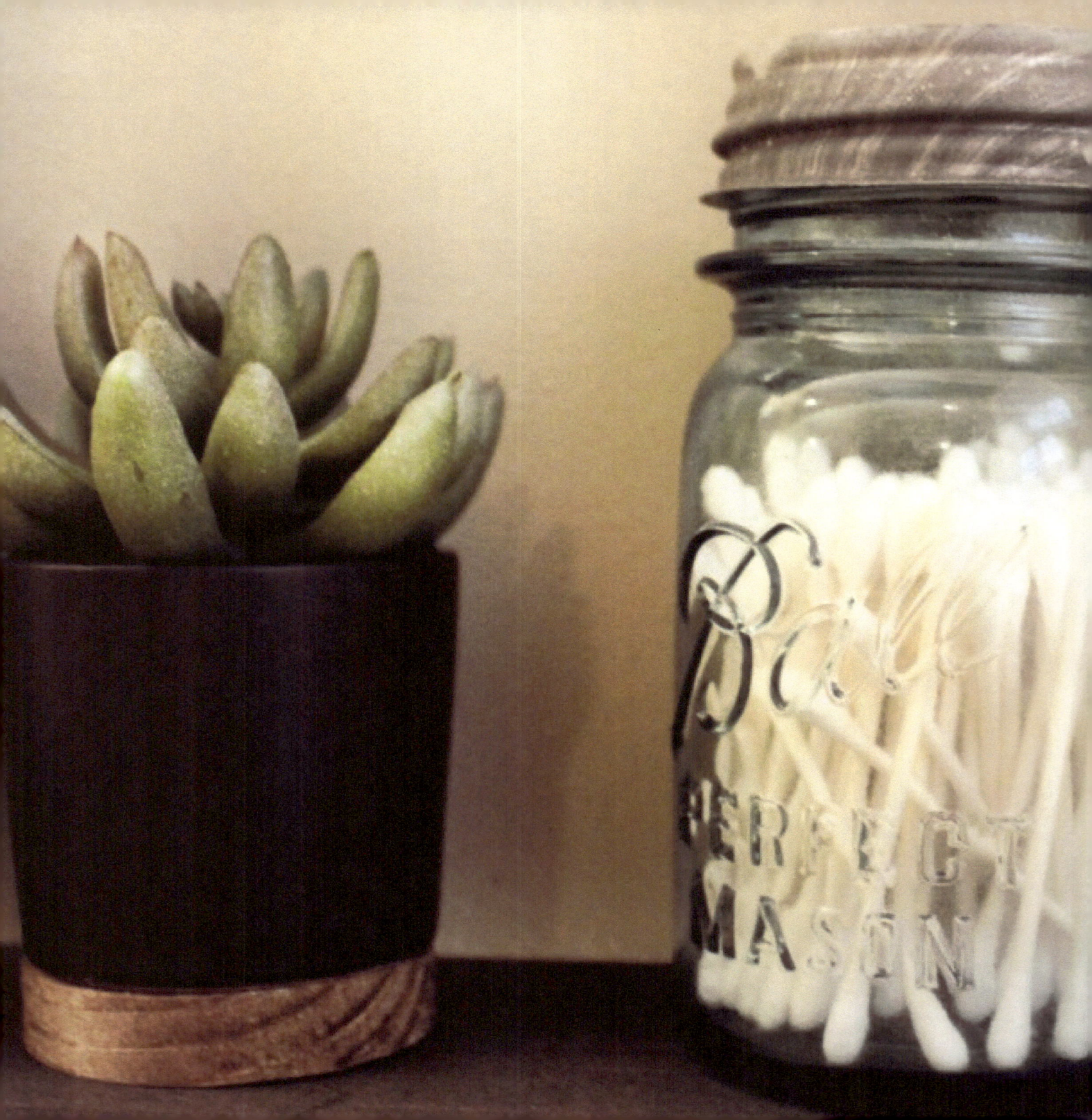

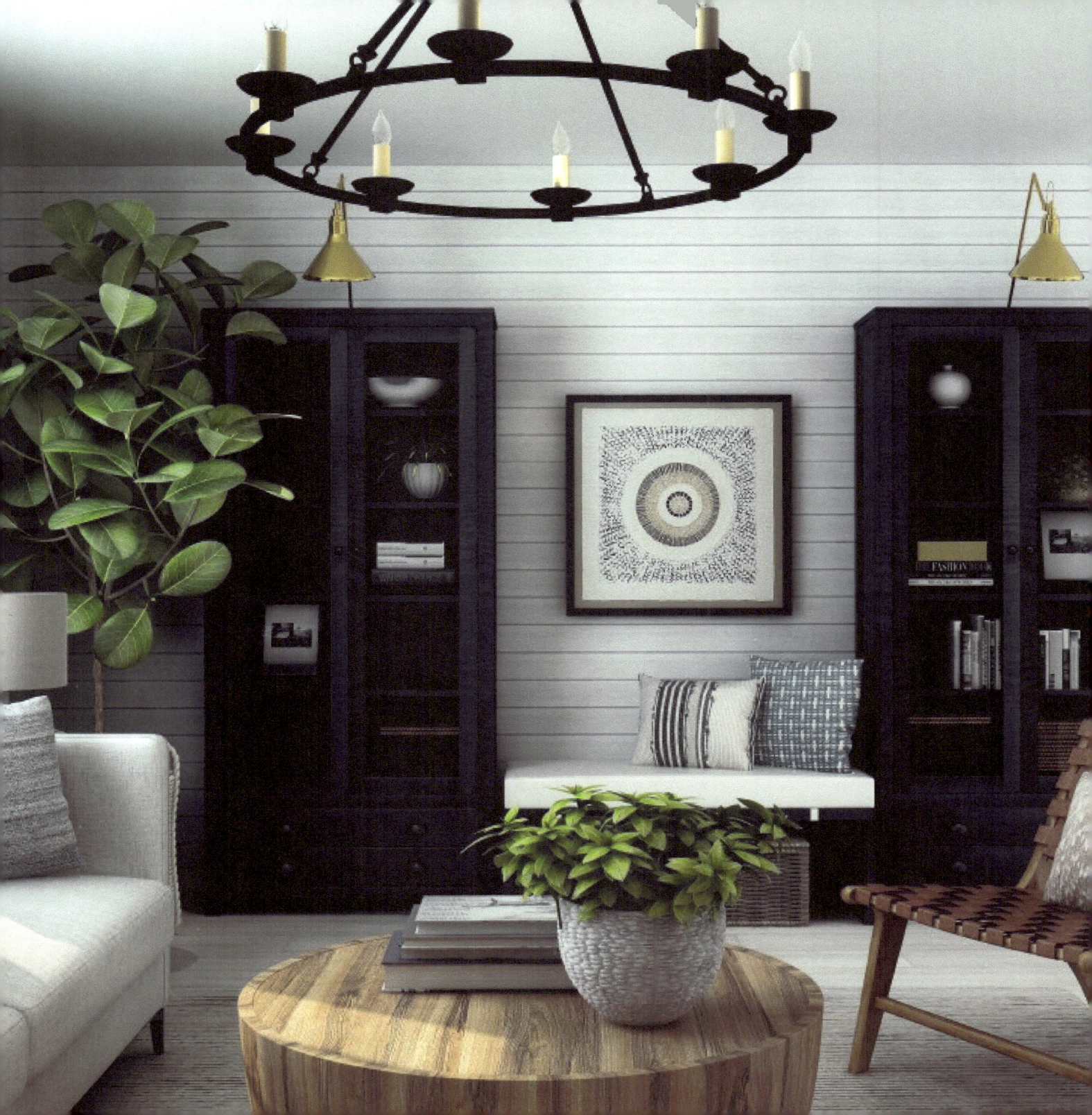

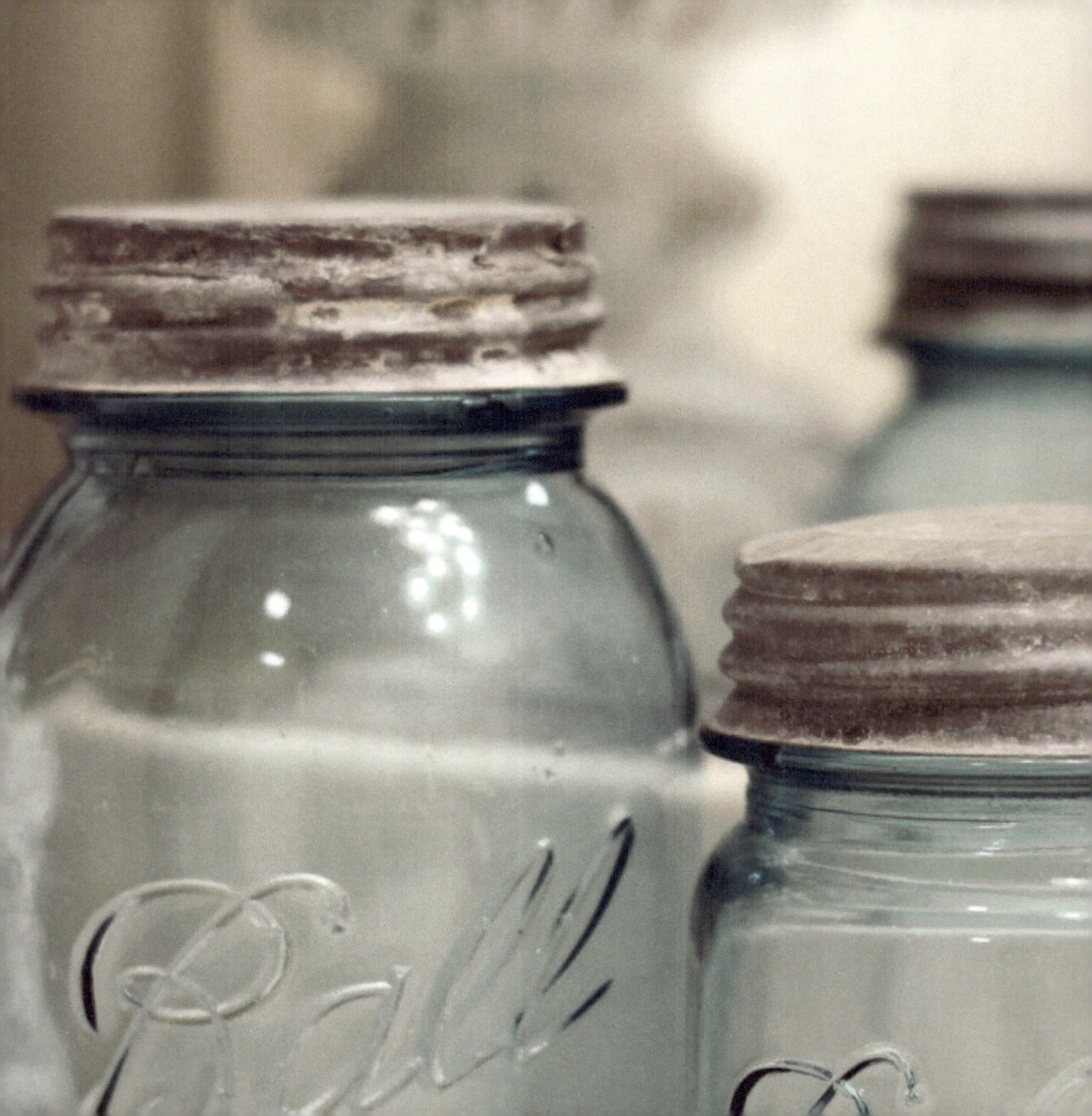

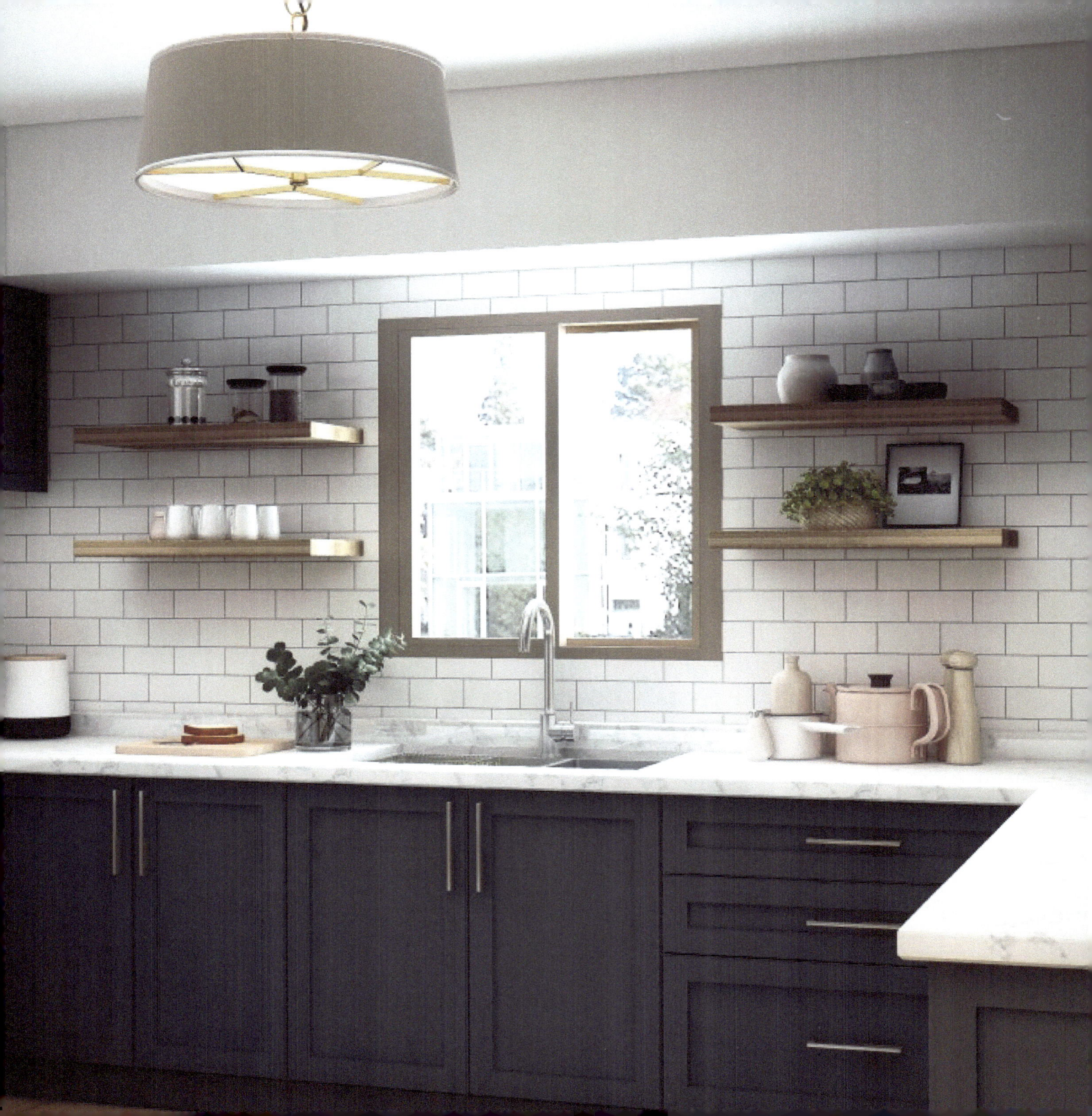

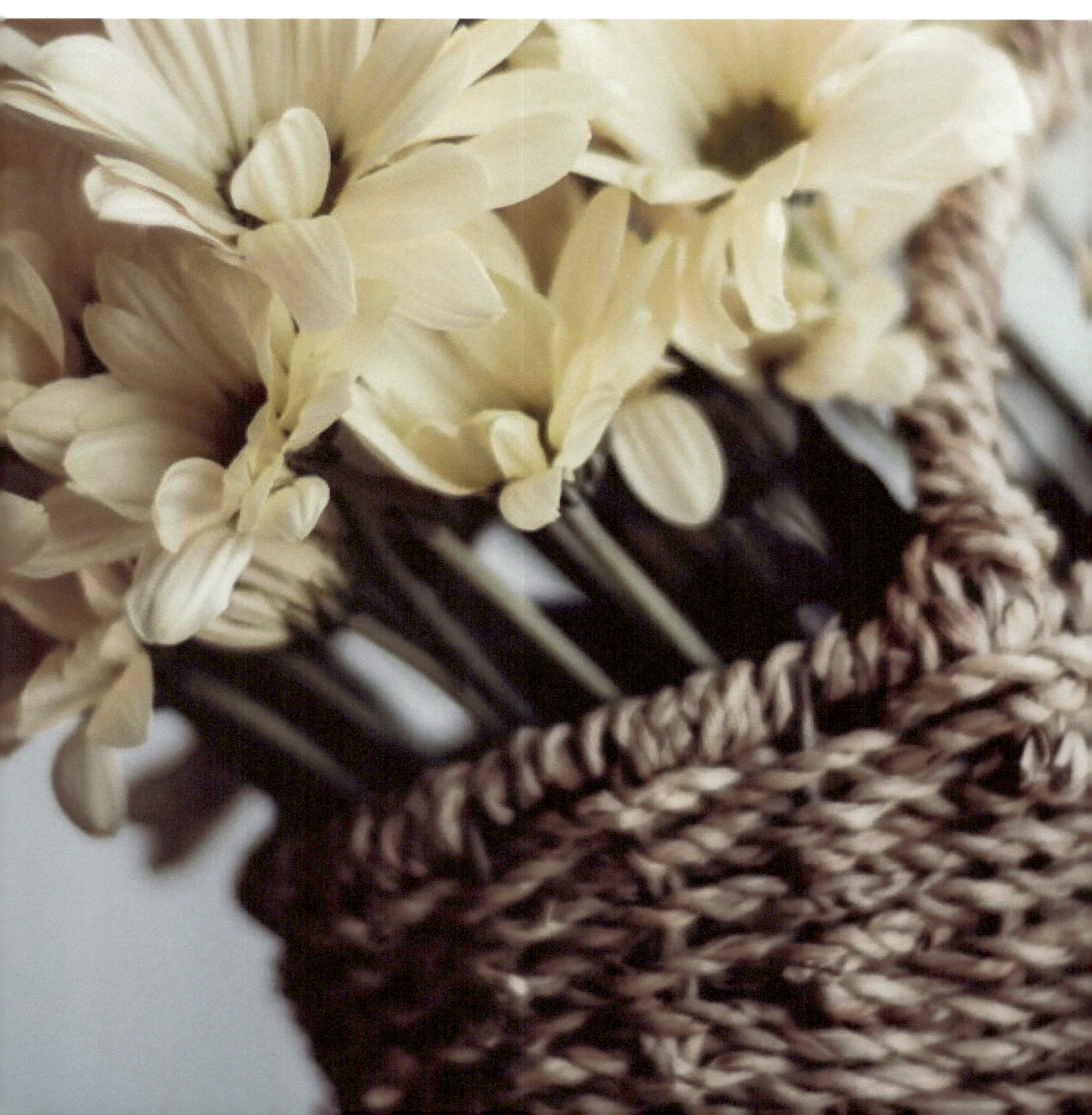

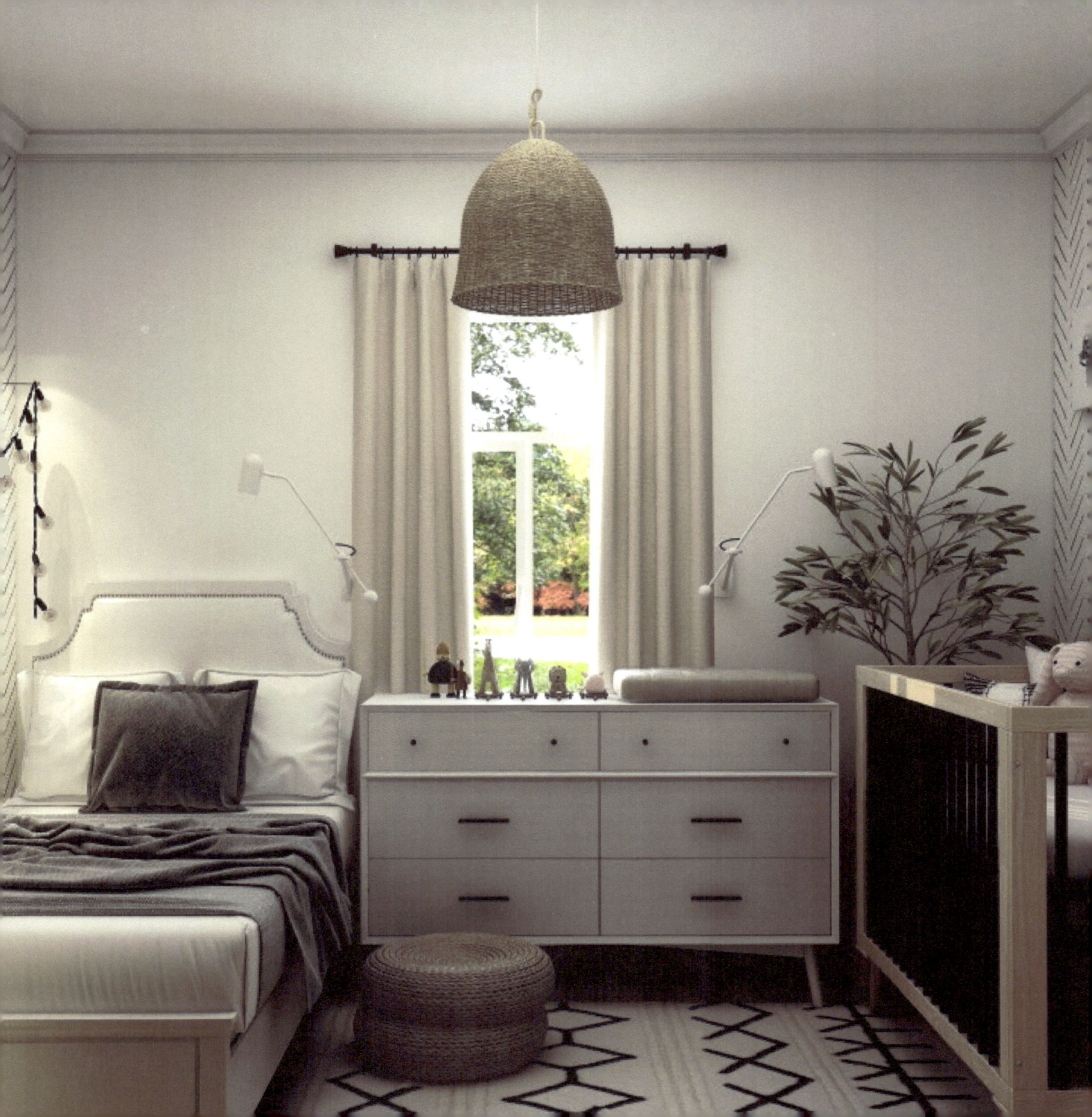

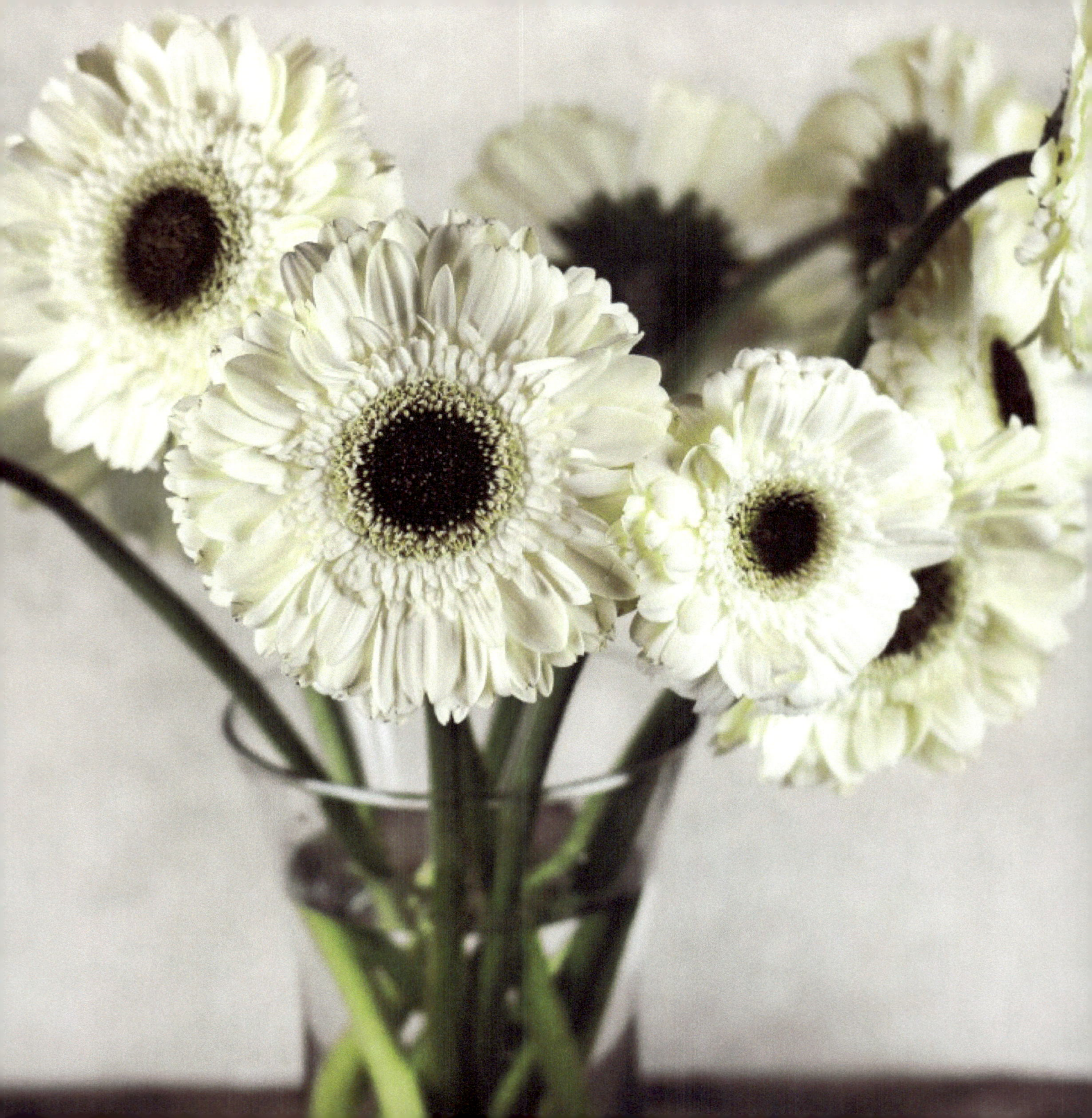

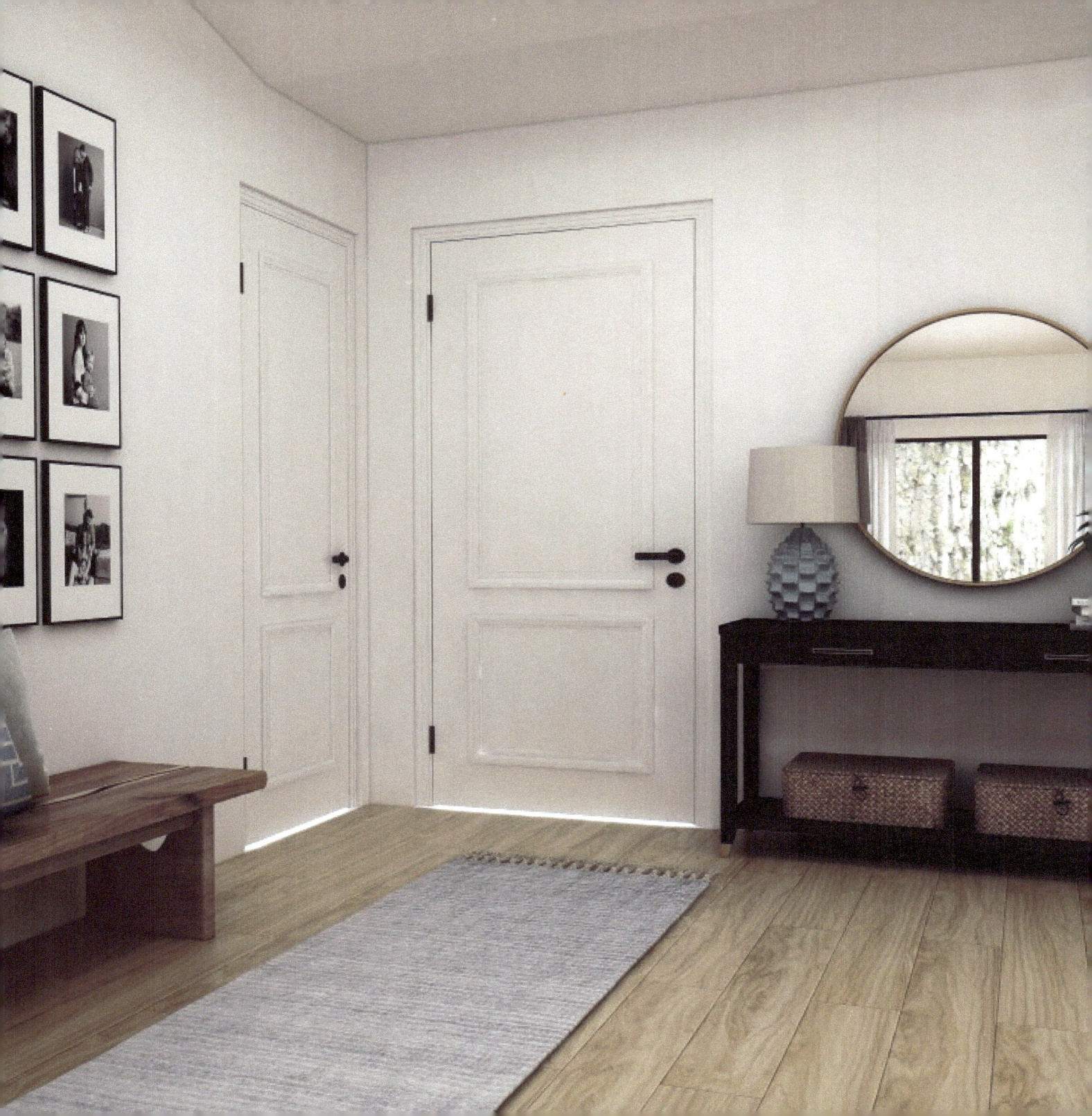

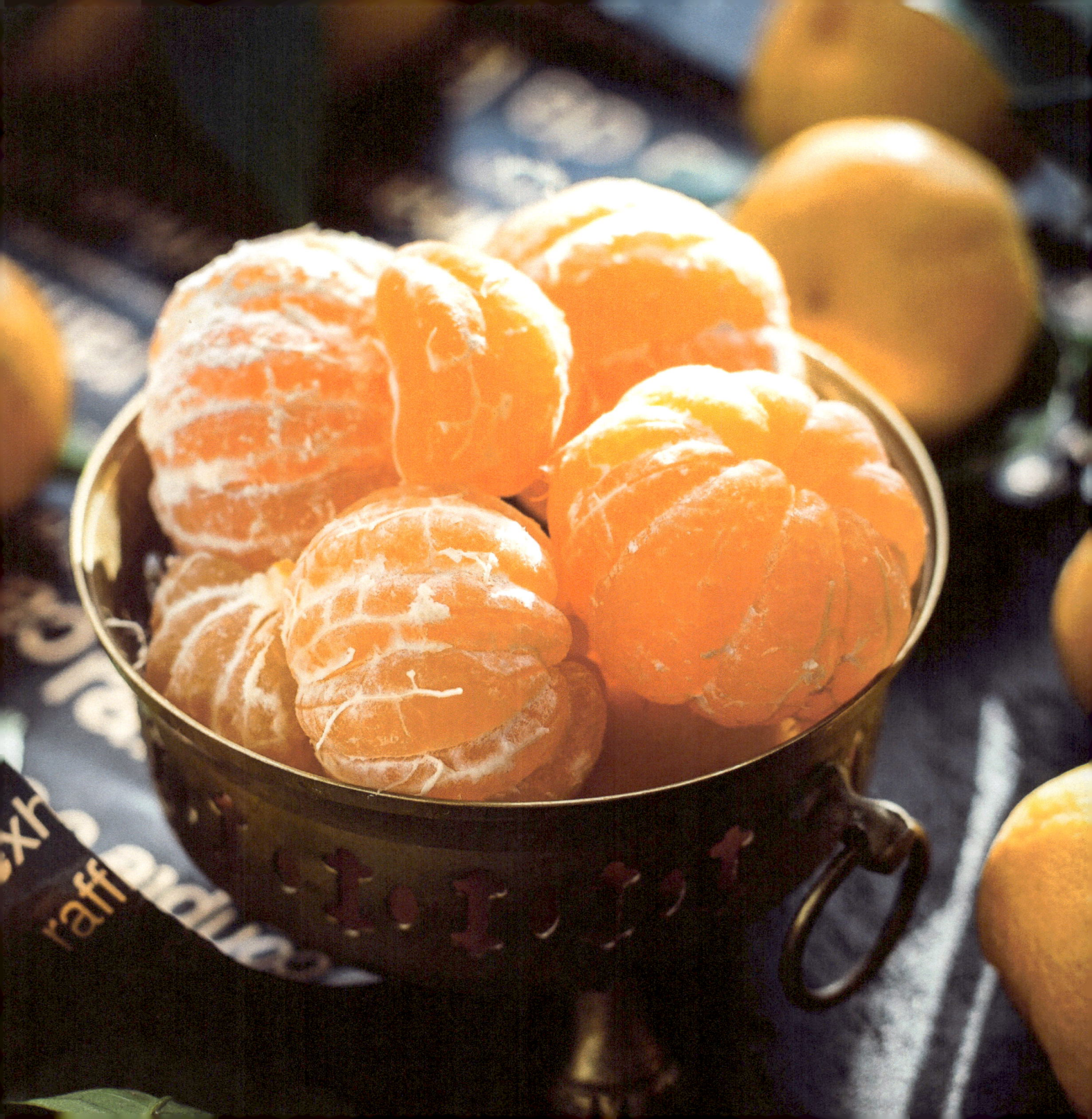

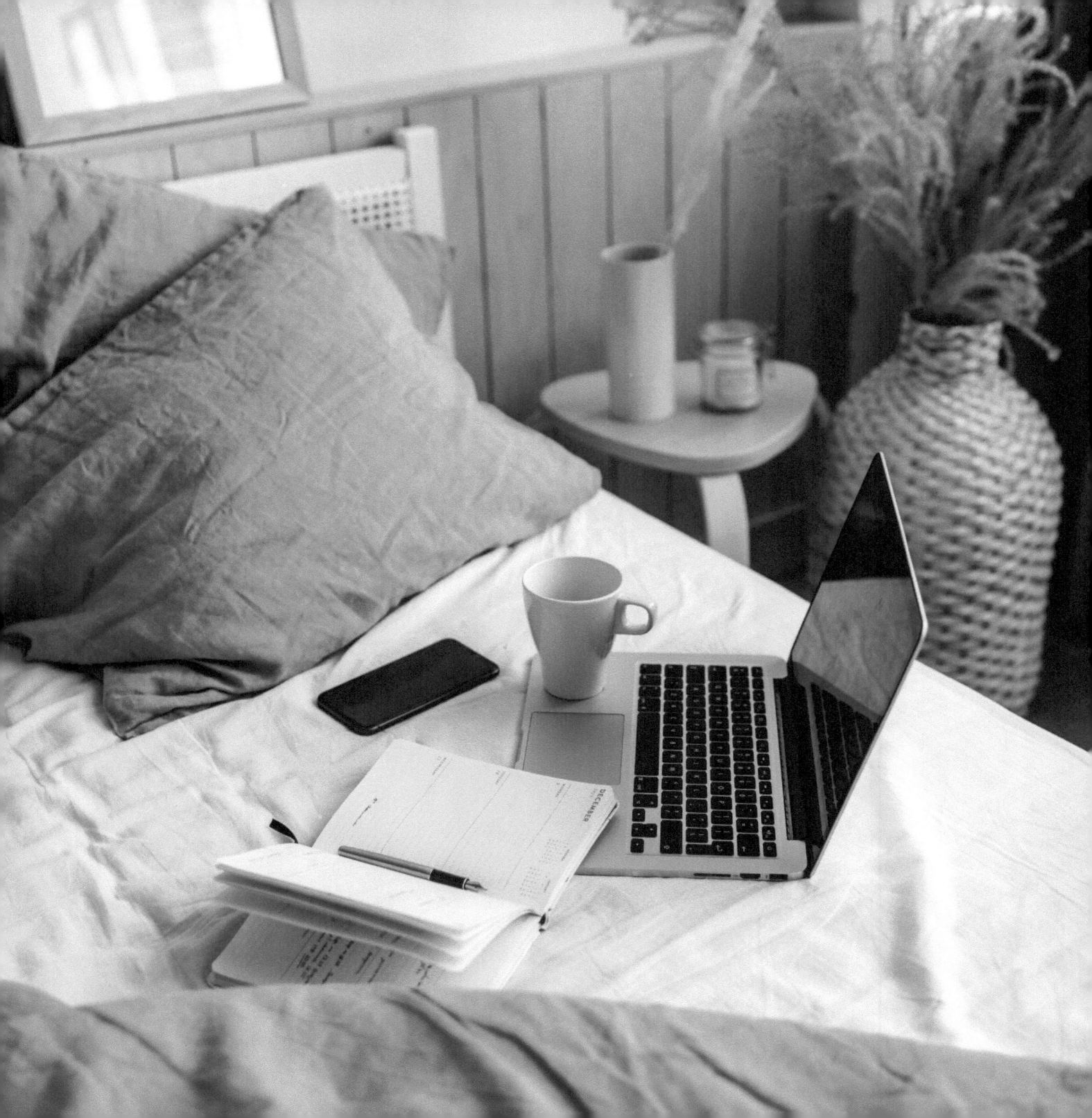

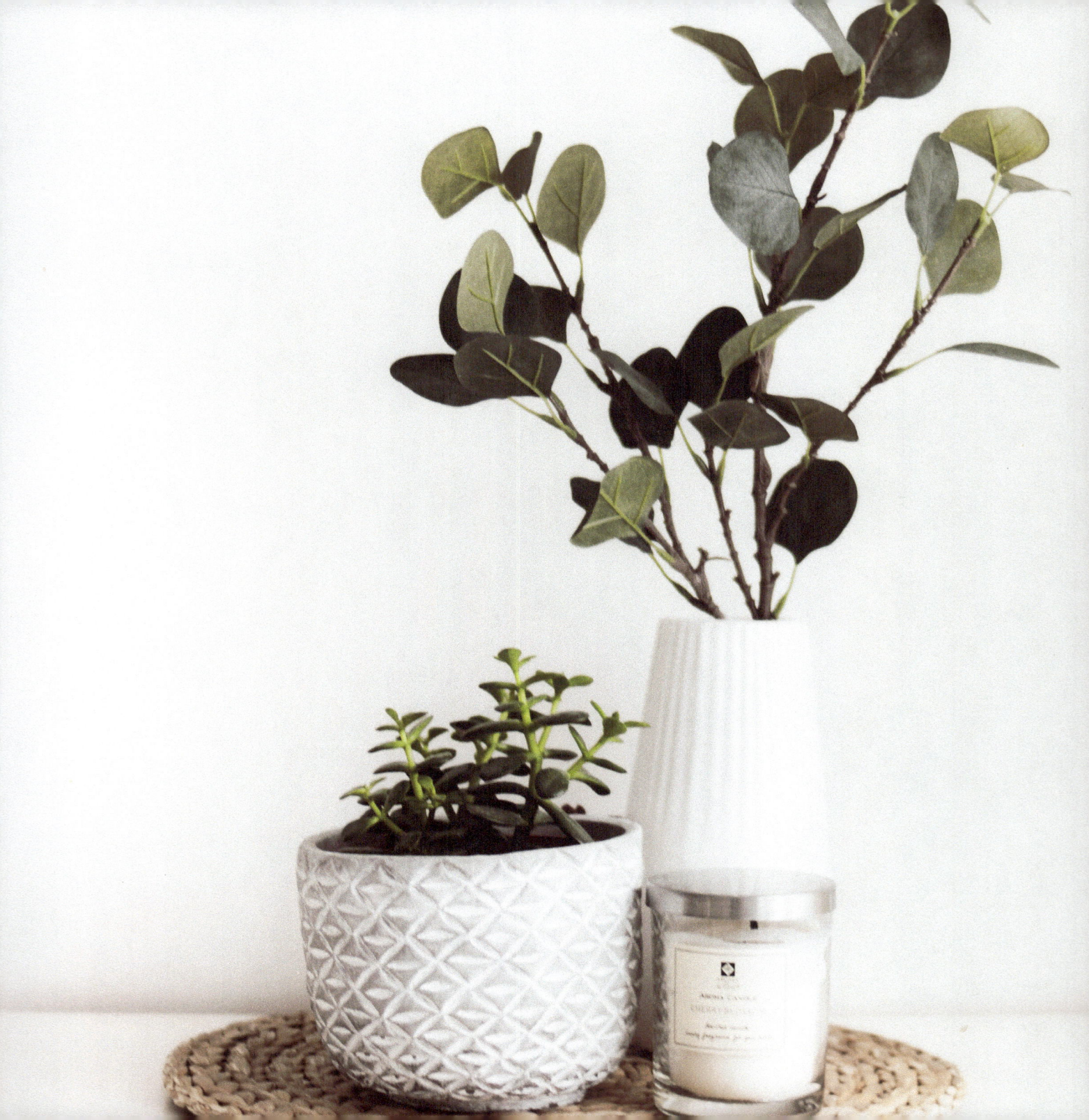

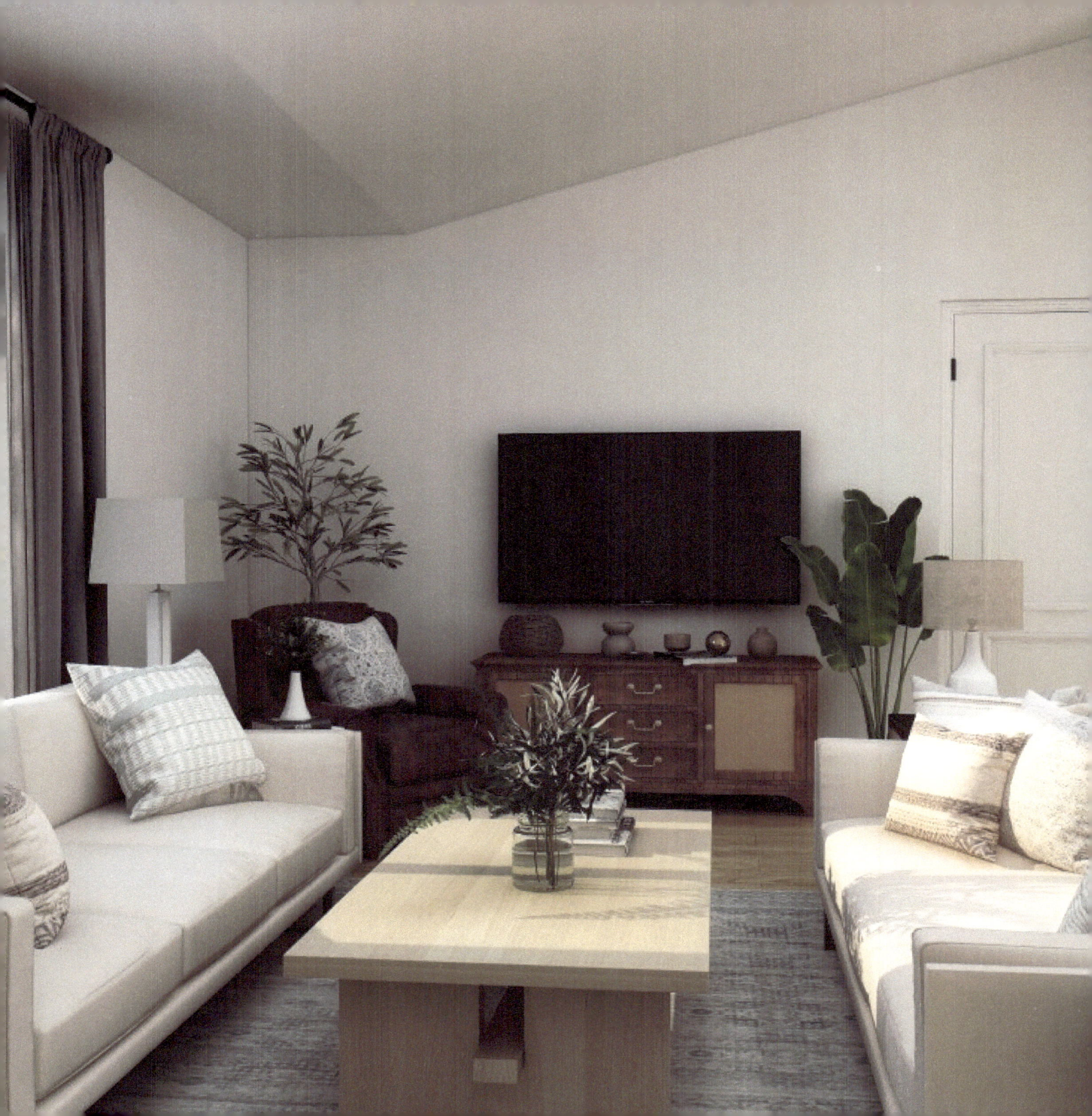

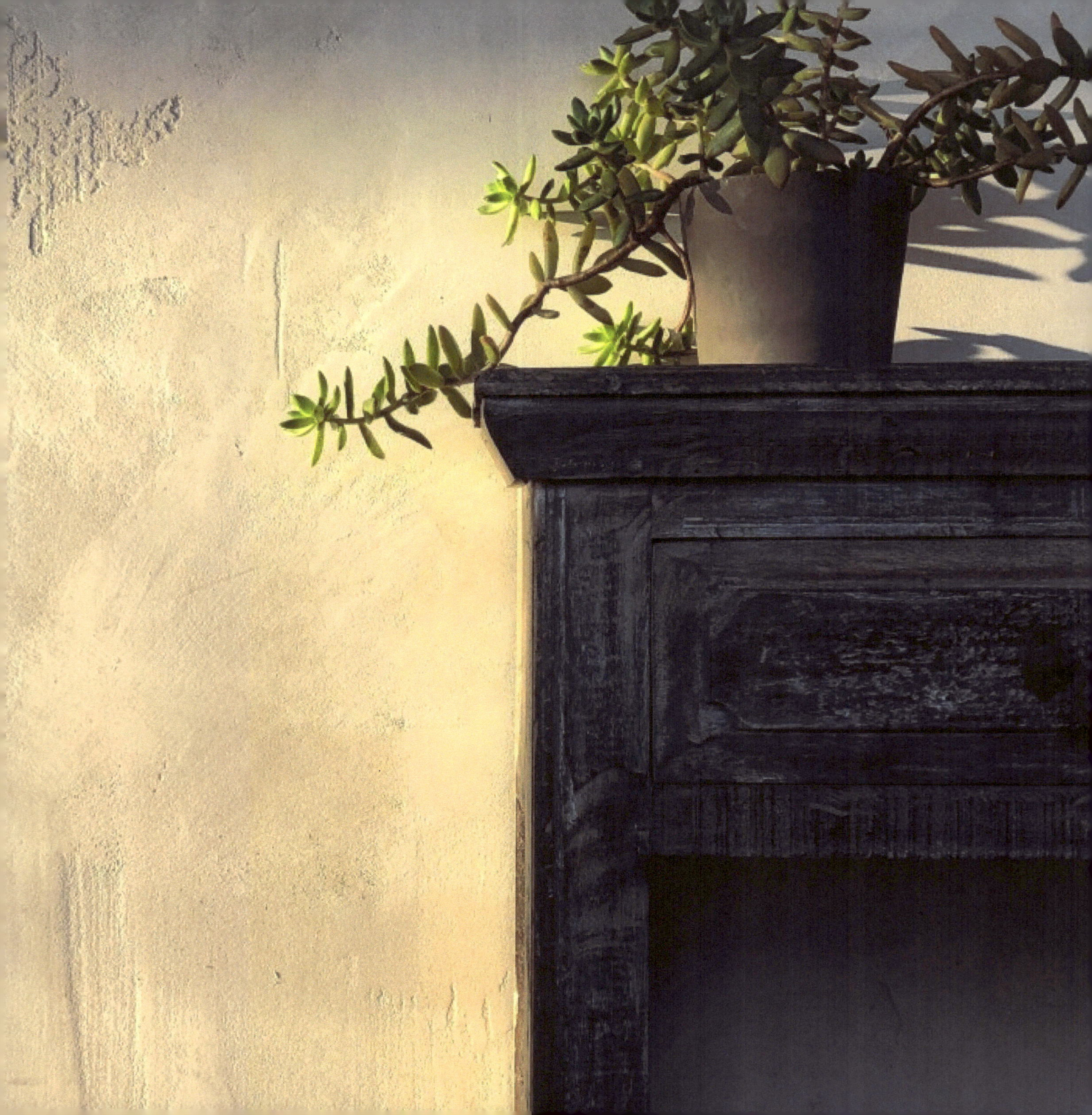

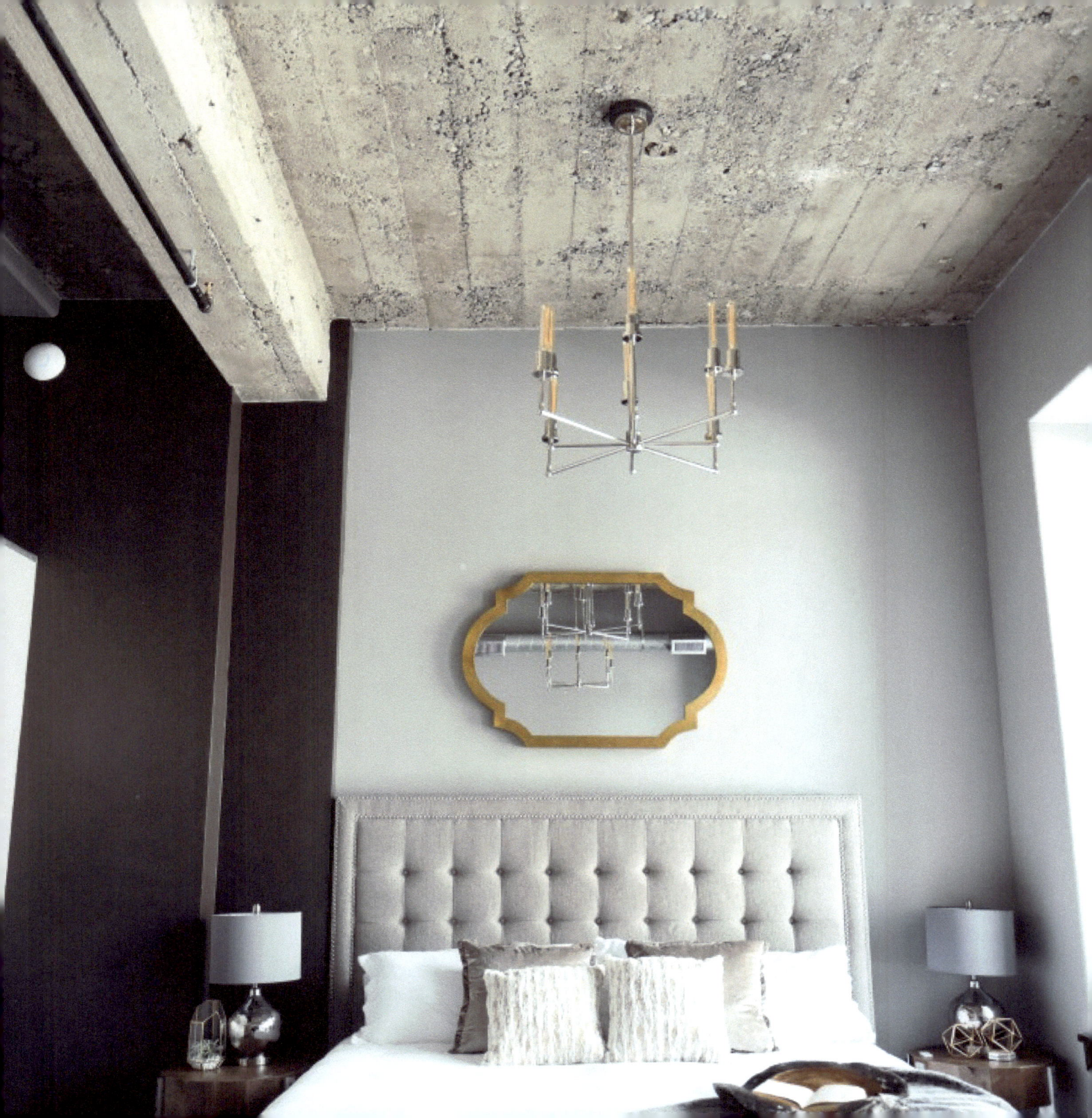

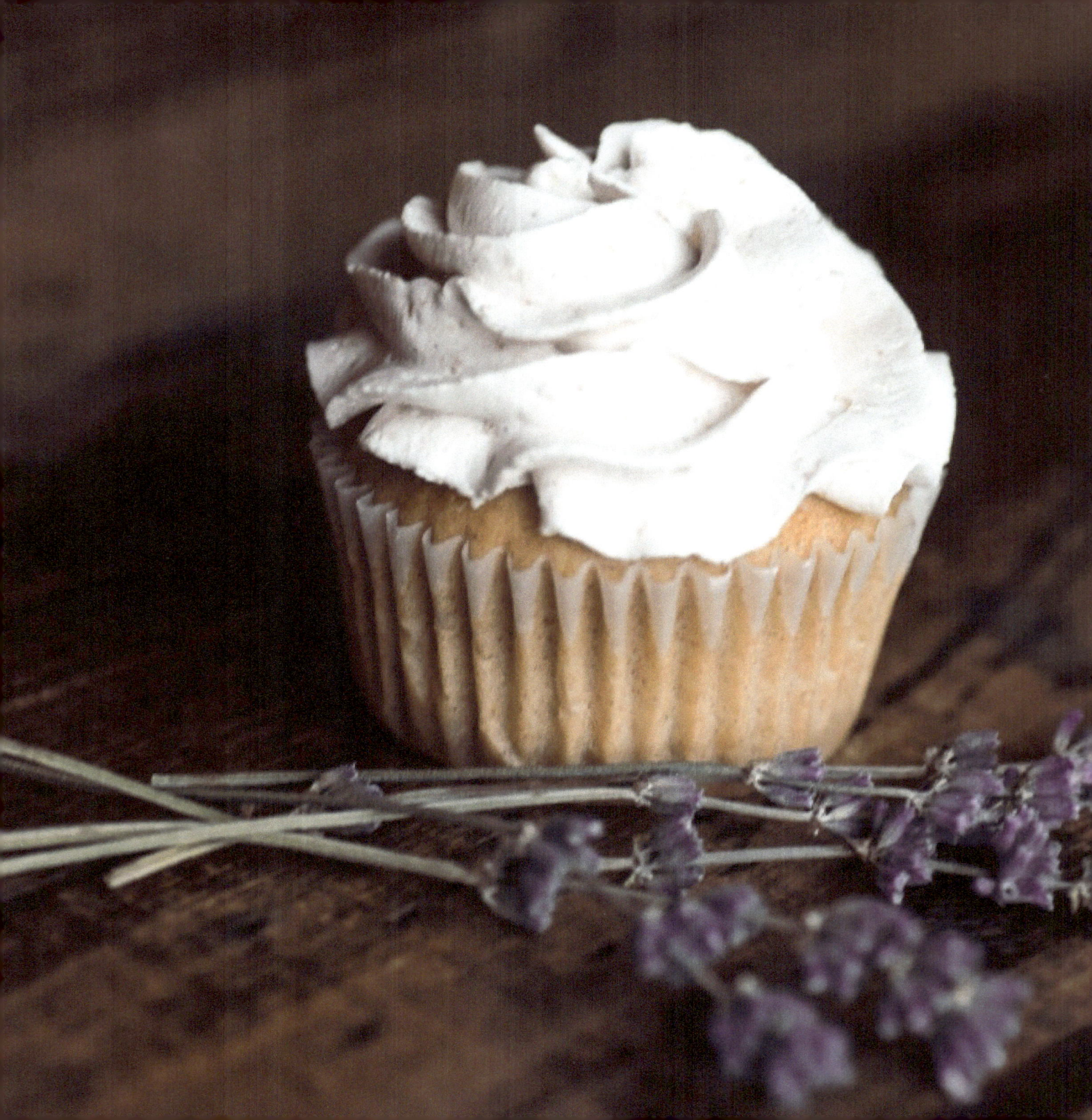

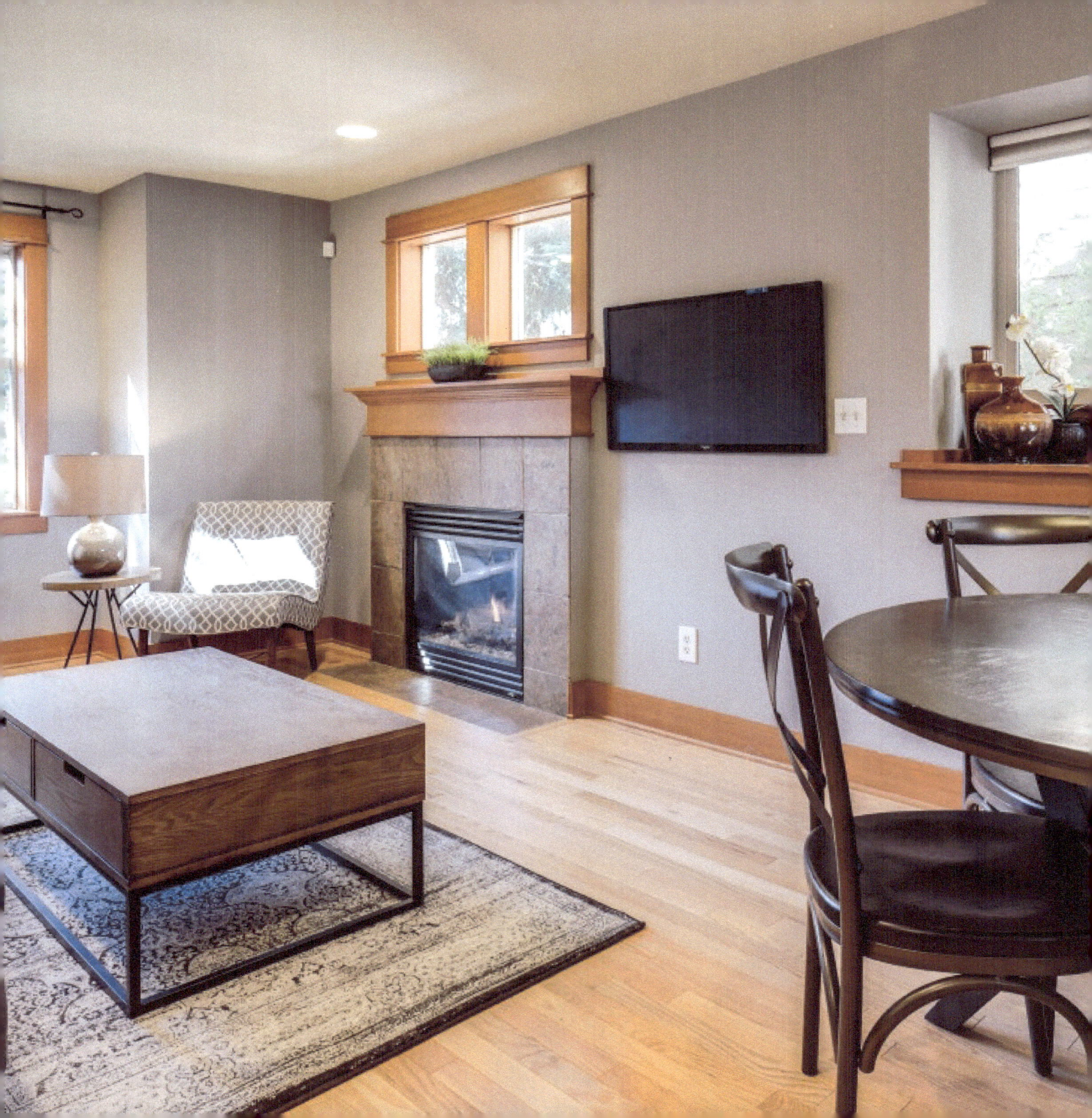

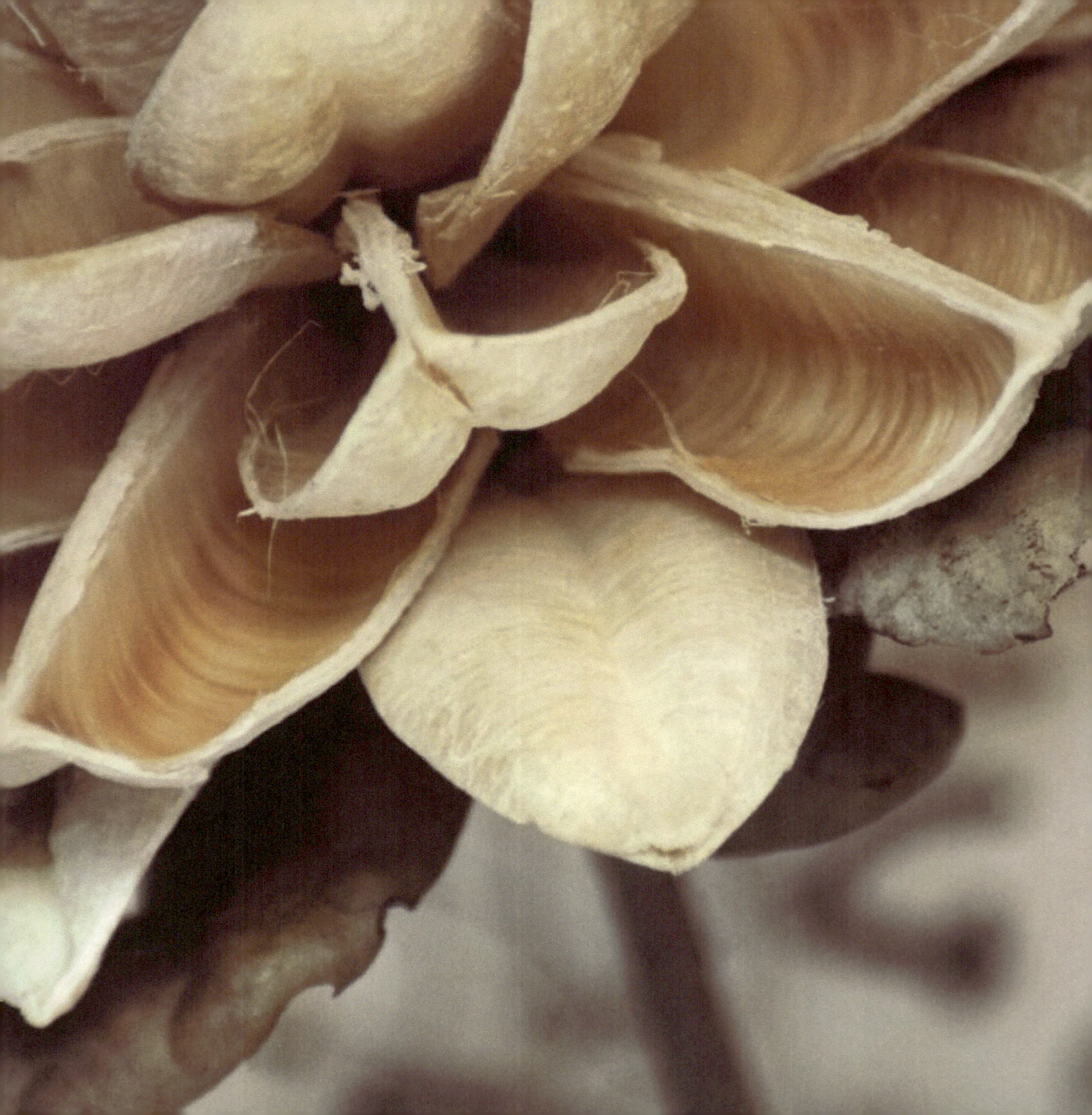

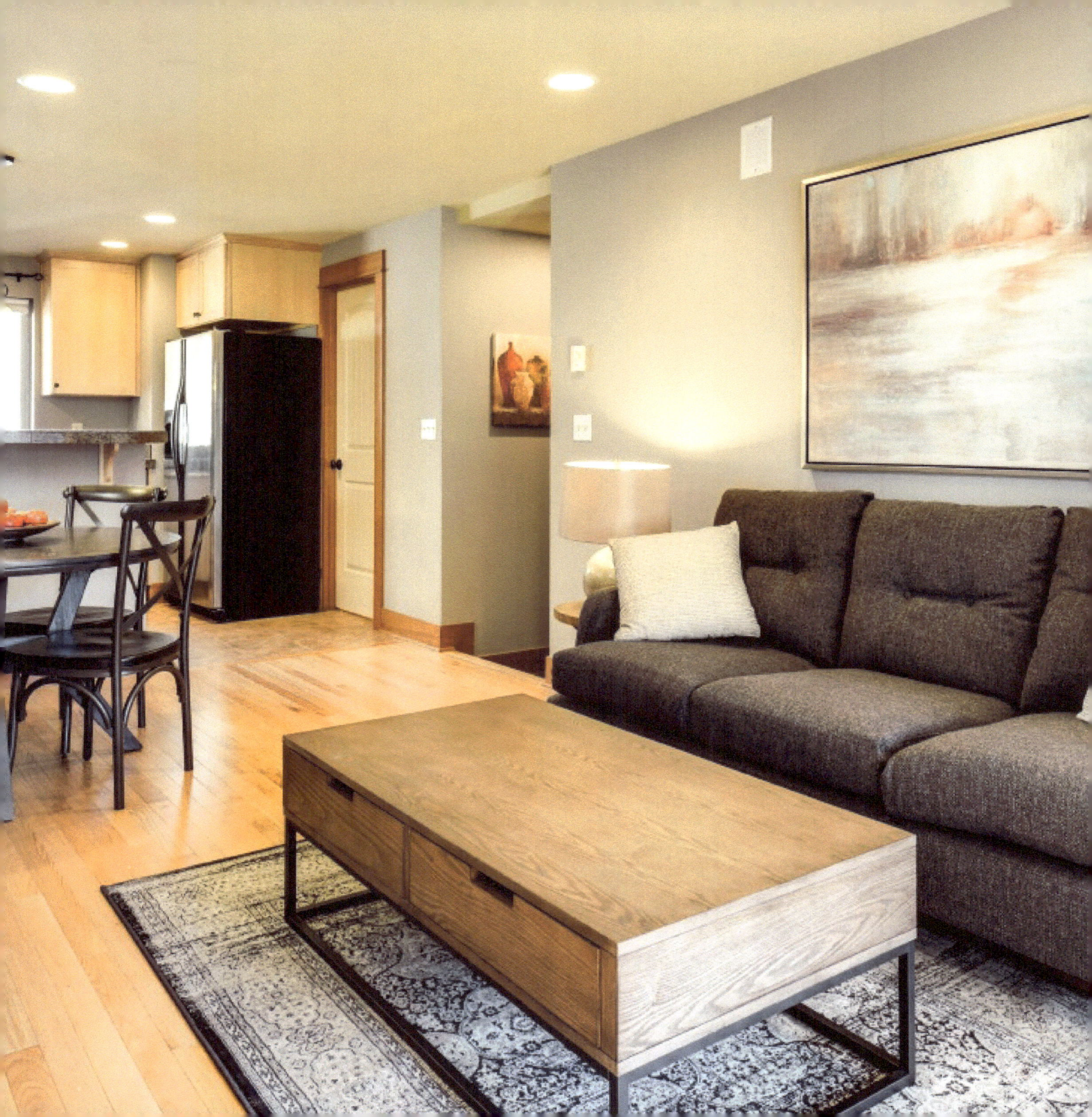

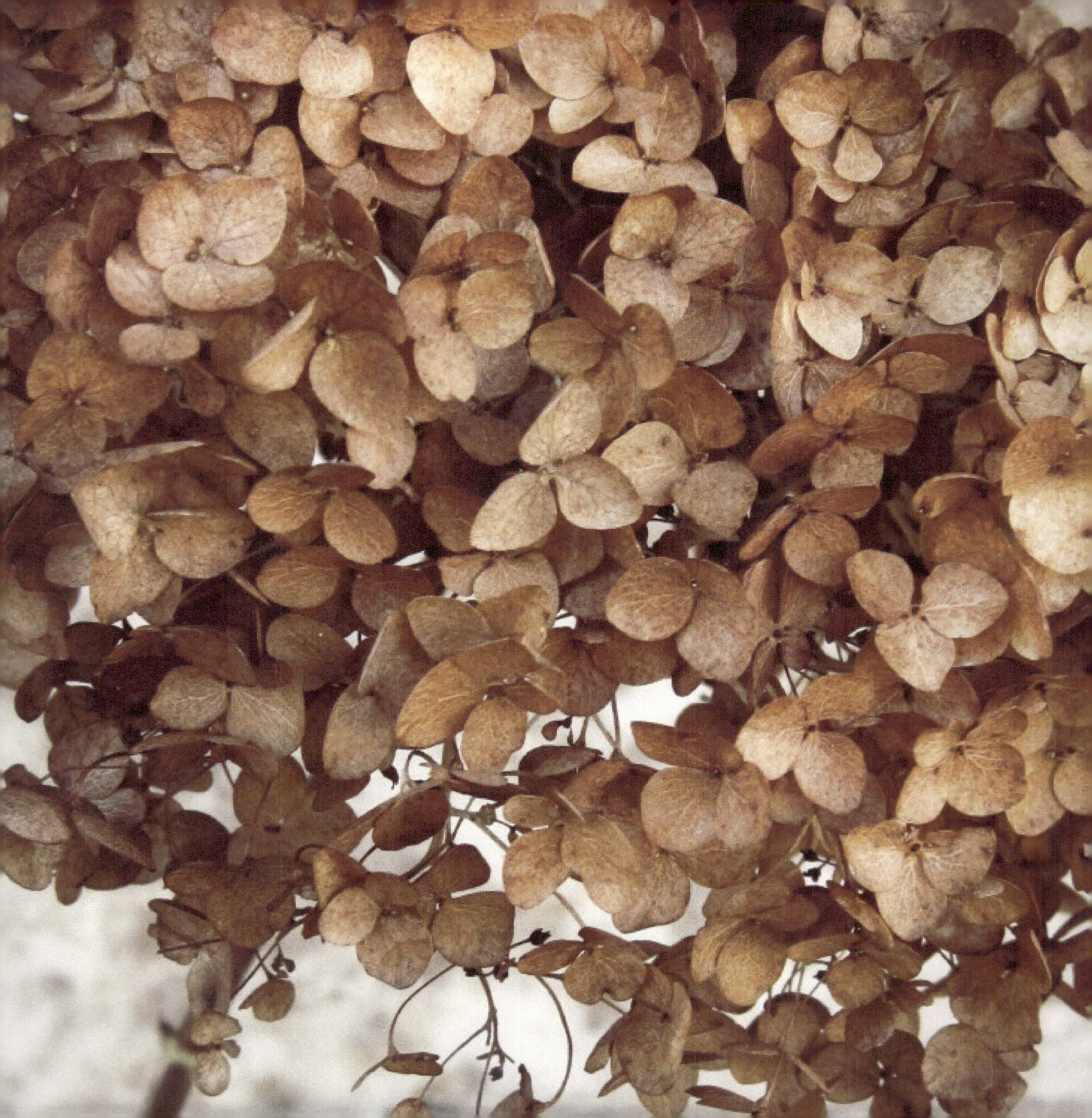

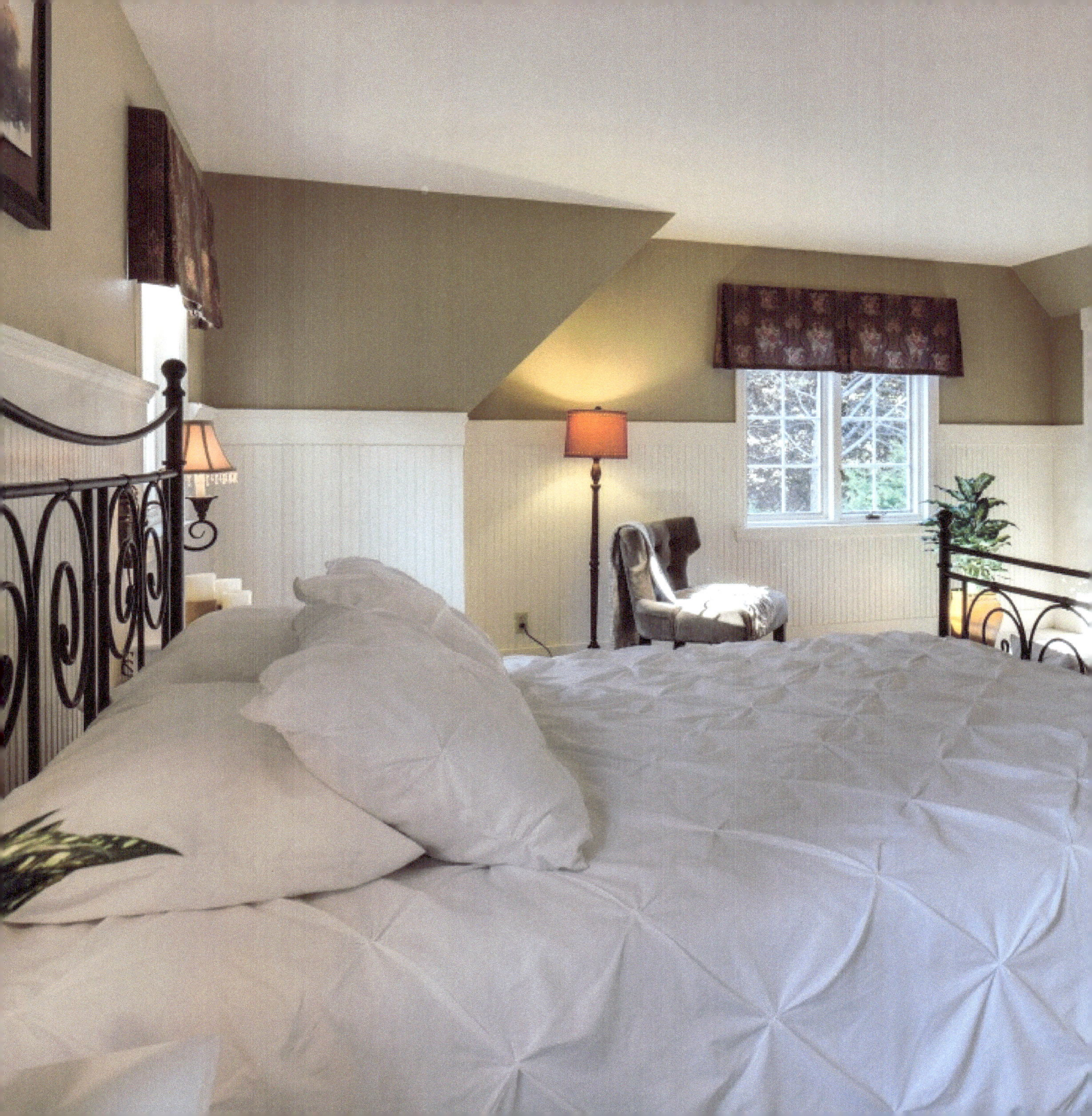

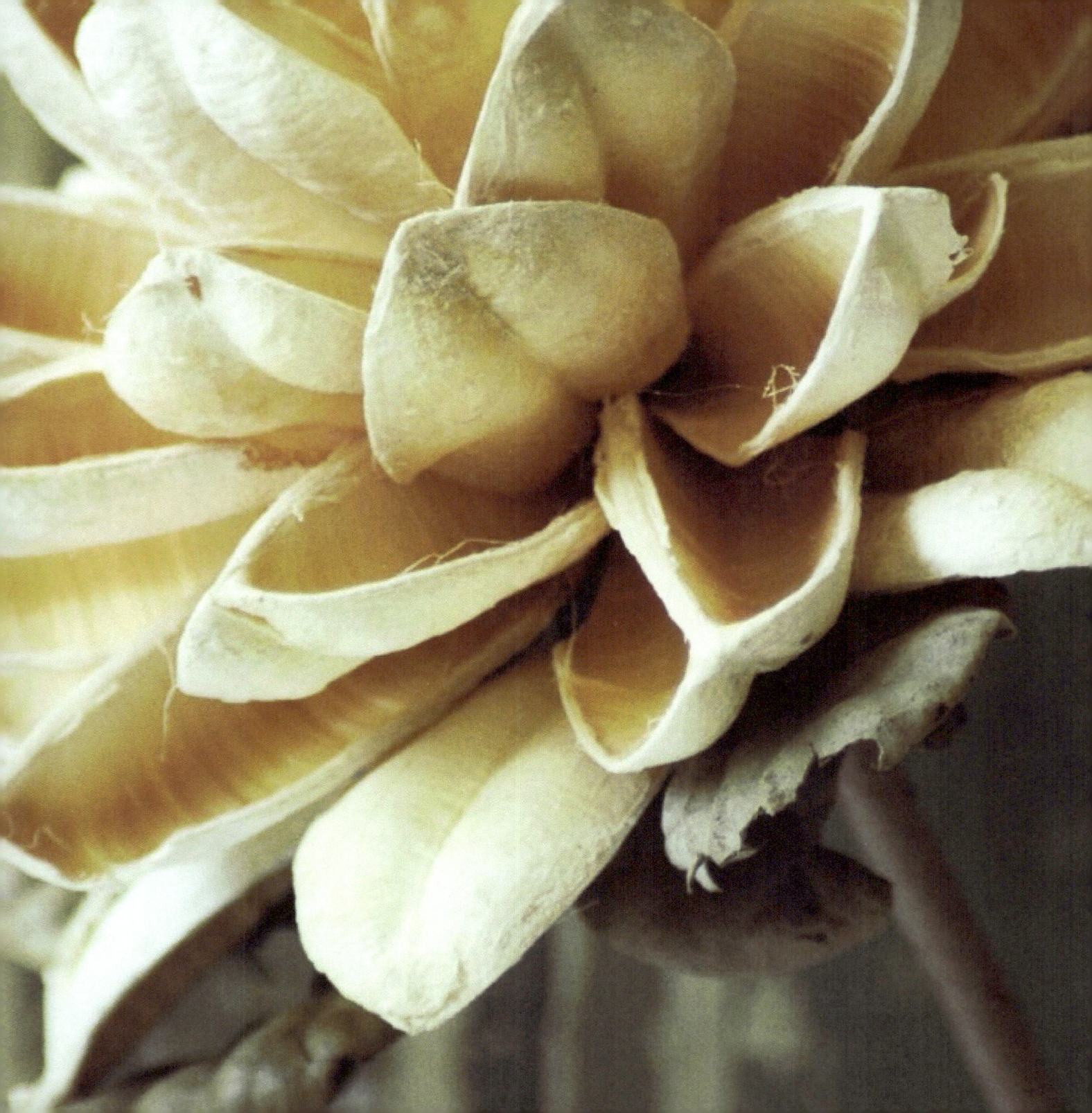

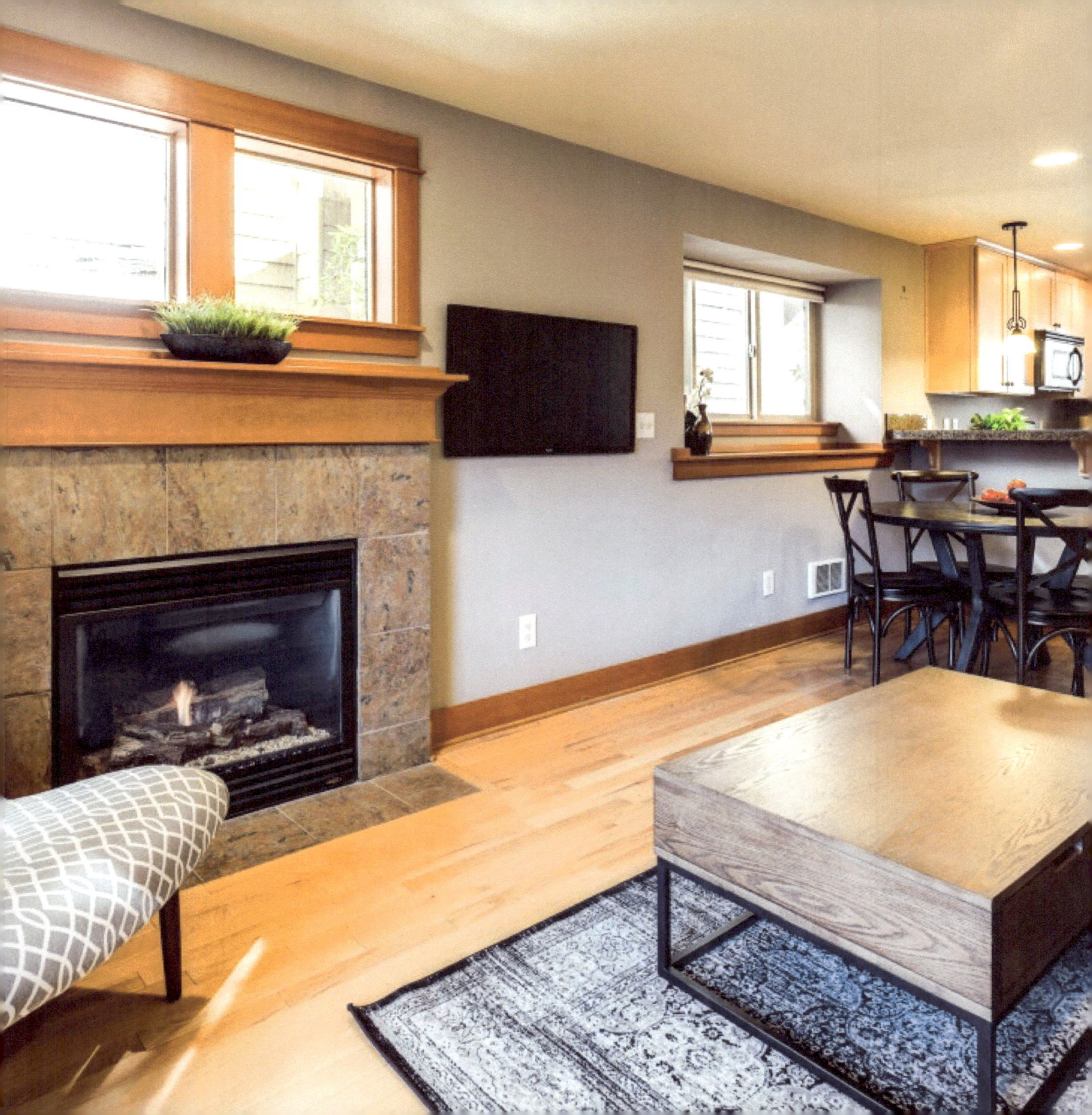

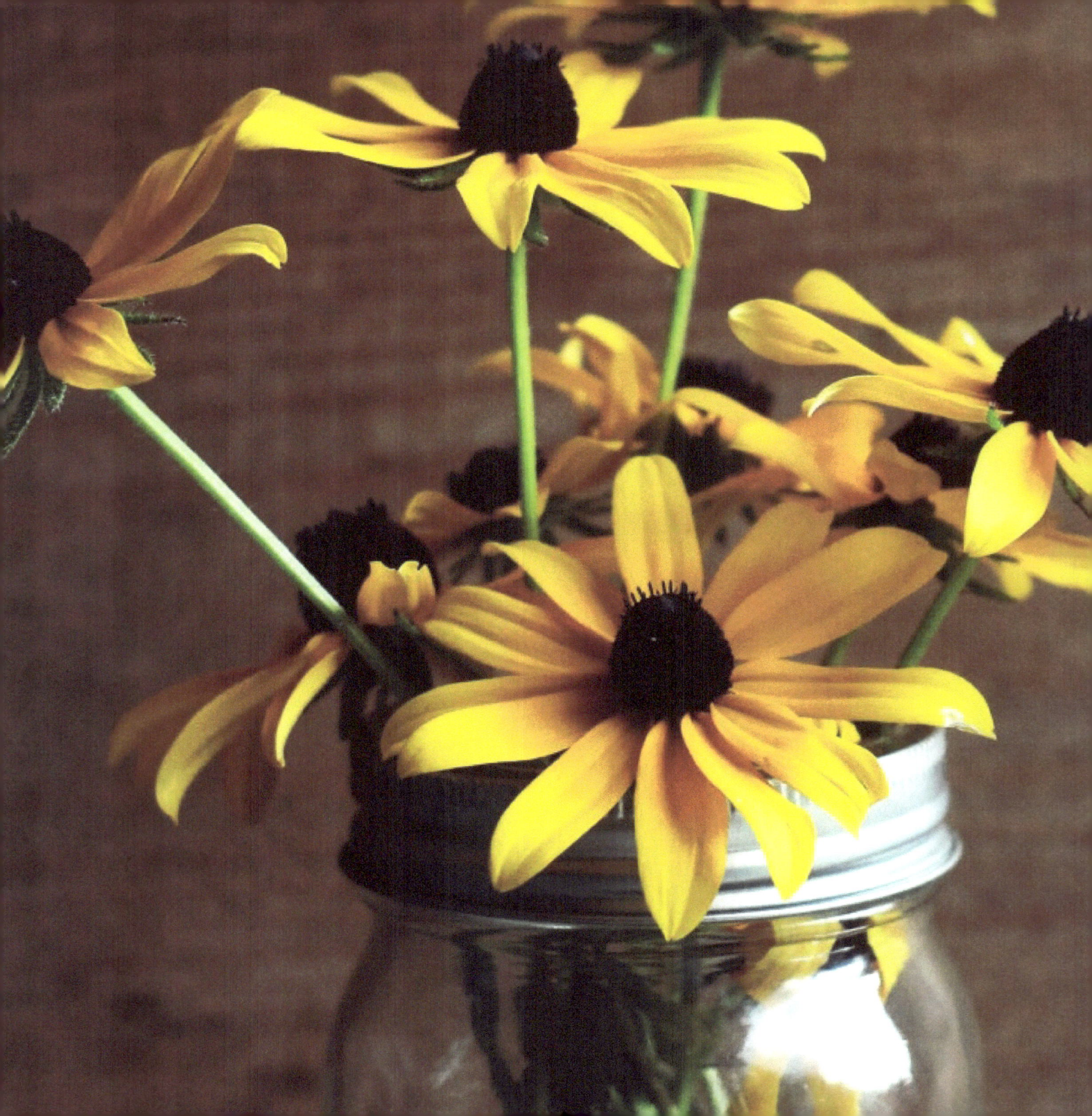

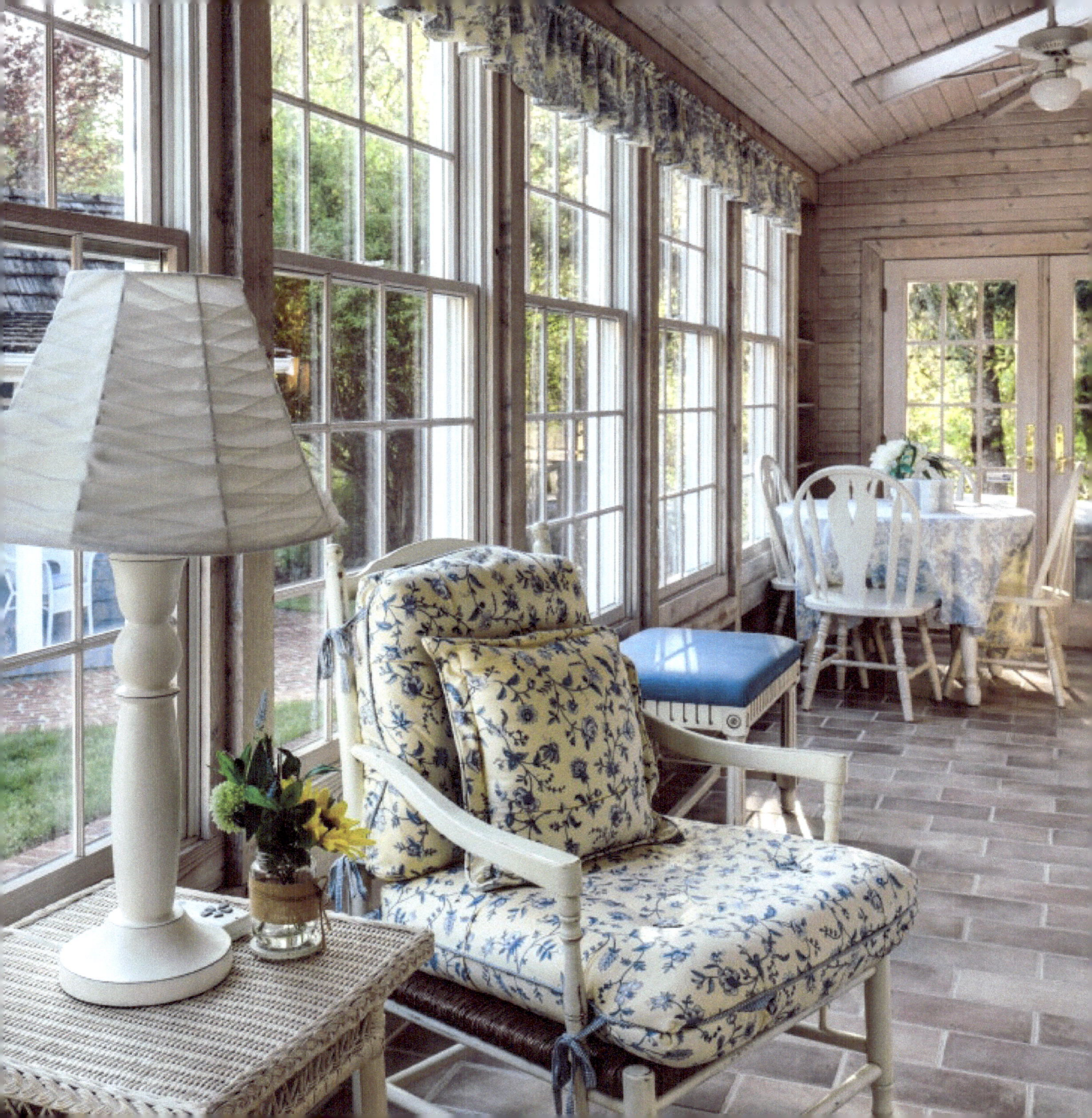

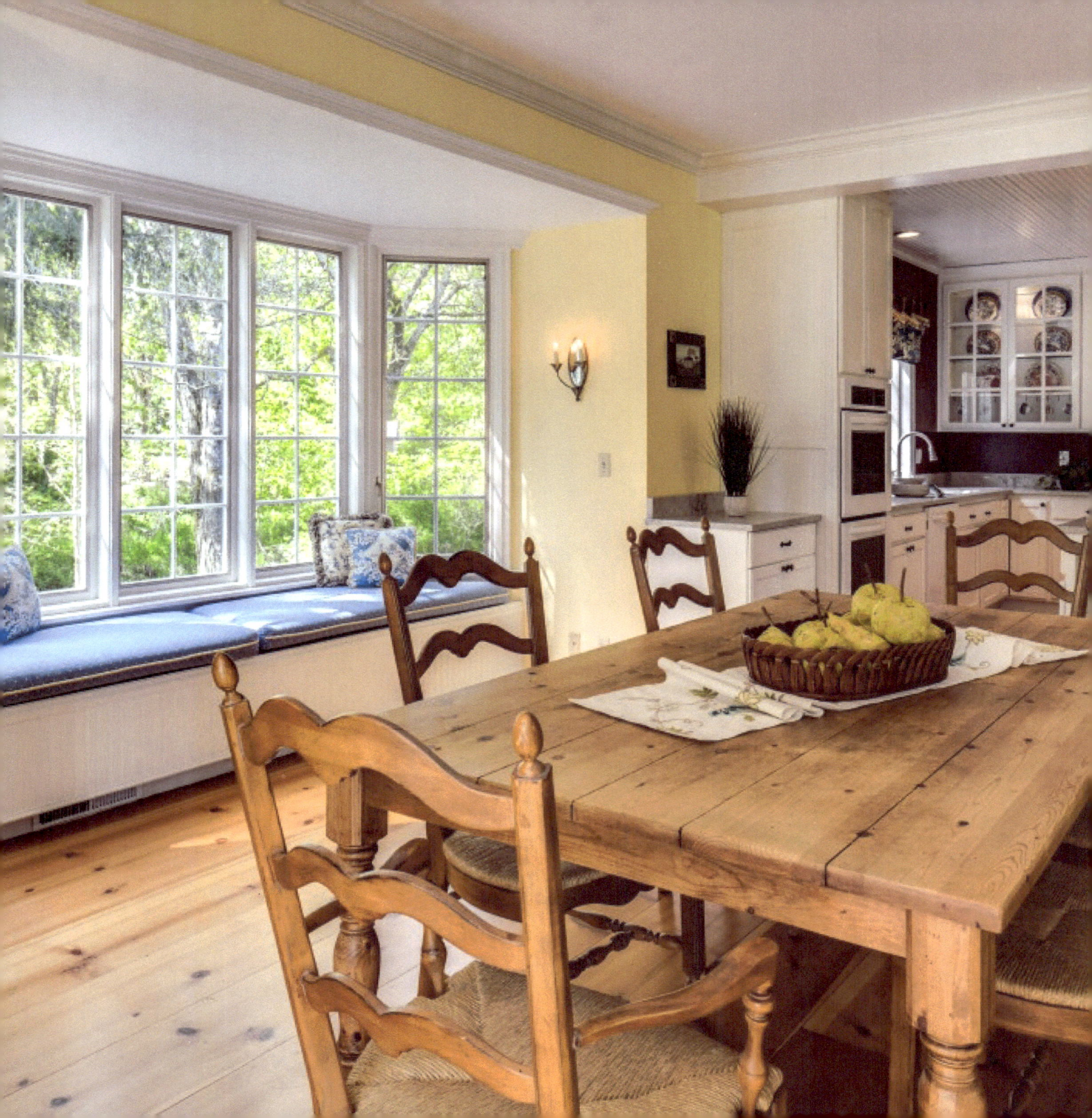

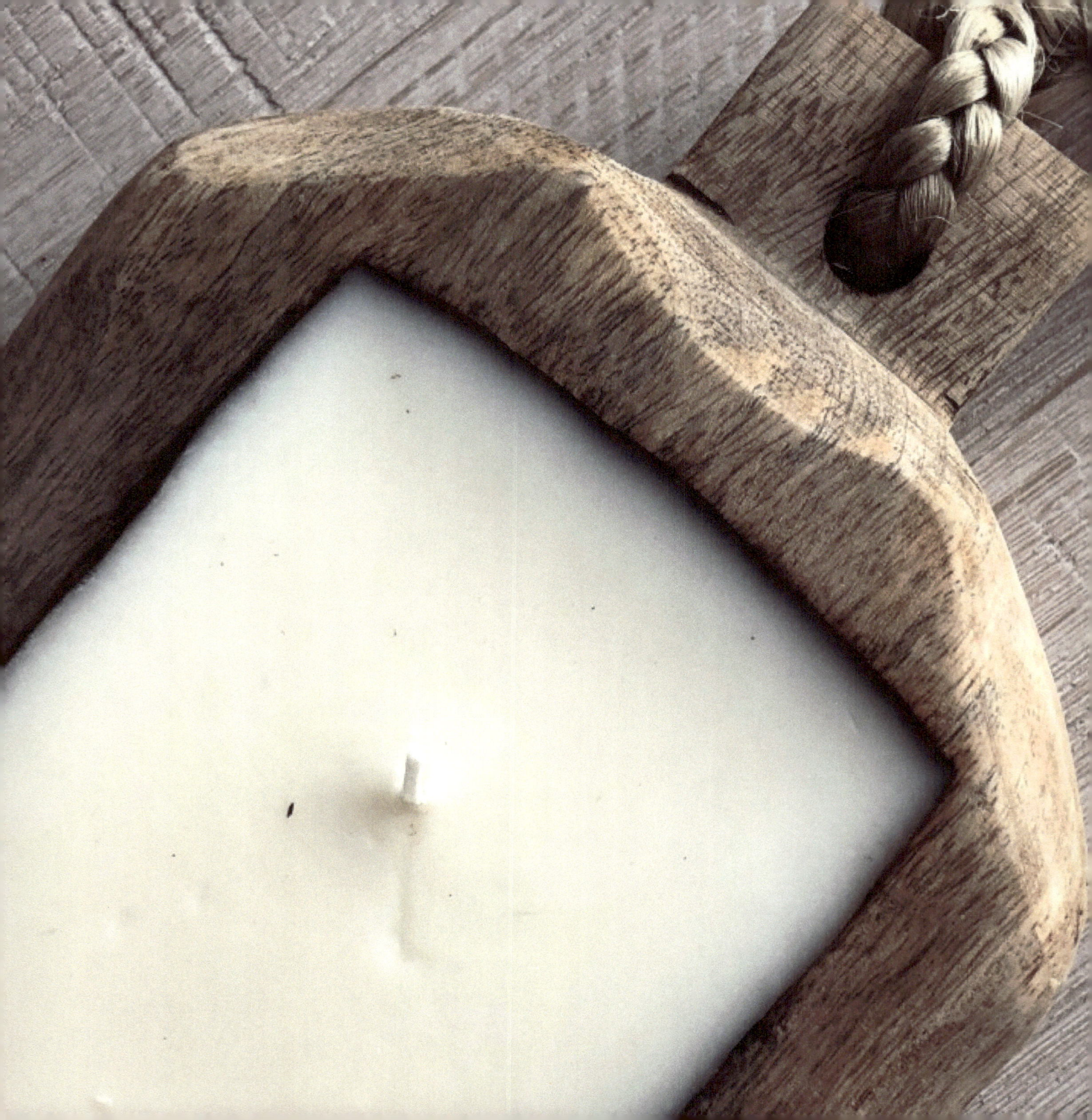

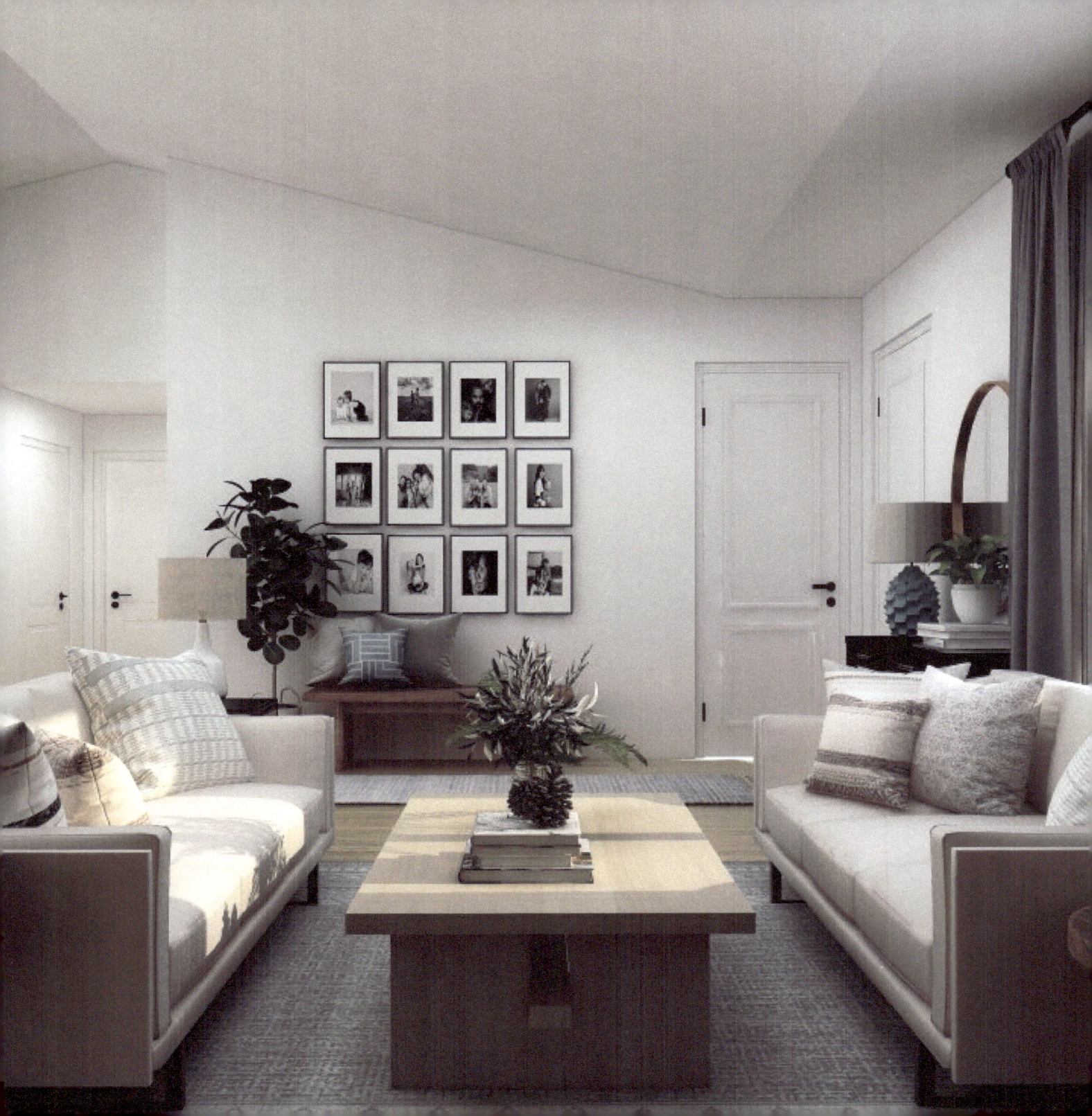

www.ingramcontent.com/pod-product-compliance
Lightning Source LLC
Chambersburg PA
CBHW040450220526
45473CB00004B/1589